D1157751

IVERSITY OF WINNIPEG
LIBRARY
515 Portage Ave.
Winnipeg, Manitoba R3B 2E9

DISCARDED

PROFESSOR DR. F. DE VRIES
LECTURES IN ECONOMICS
Theory, Institutions, Policy

VOLUME 4

NORTH-HOLLAND PUBLISHING COMPANY
AMSTERDAM · NEW YORK · OXFORD

ECONOMIC, LEGAL, AND POLITICAL
DIMENSIONS OF COMPETITION

HB
238
.D45
1982

ECONOMIC, LEGAL, AND POLITICAL DIMENSIONS OF COMPETITION

HAROLD DEMSETZ

University of California, Los Angeles

1982

NORTH-HOLLAND PUBLISHING COMPANY
AMSTERDAM · NEW YORK · OXFORD

© NORTH-HOLLAND PUBLISHING COMPANY - 1982

All rights reserved. No part of this publication may be reproduced, stored in a retrieval system, or transmitted, in any form or by any means, electronic, mechanical, photocopying, recording or otherwise, without the prior permission of the copyright owner.

Publishers:
NORTH-HOLLAND PUBLISHING COMPANY
AMSTERDAM · NEW YORK · OXFORD

Sole distributors for the U.S.A. and Canada:
ELSEVIER SCIENCE PUBLISHING COMPANY INC.
52 VANDERBILT AVENUE, NEW YORK, N.Y. 10017

ISBN 0-444-86442-3

PRINTED IN THE NETHERLANDS

Professor F. de Vries (1884–1958) became the first professor of economics at the Netherlands School of Economics (Rotterdam), which was founded in 1913. In 1945 he accepted an offer of the University of Amsterdam to teach economics in its Faculty of Law. On the occasion of his 70th birthday, May 2; 1954, his pupils created the Professor F. de Vries Foundation to honour a most influential teacher and a scholar of outstanding theoretical and practical wisdom.

The aim of the foundation is to regularly invite prominent economists from abroad for a series of lectures on theoretical subjects, as a stimulus to theoretical work in economics in the Netherlands.

CONTENTS

Lecture 1

Prologue. **THE PRESUMPTION OF COMPETITION**

I. A Puzzle About Competition

Competition occupies so important a position in economics that it is difficult to imagine economics as a social discipline without it.   Stripped of competition, economics would consist largely of the maximizing calculus of an isolated Robinson Crusoe economy. Few economists complete a major work without referring to competition, and the classical economists found in competition a source of regularity and scientific propositions. Adam Smith relies on it to bring market prices to their "natural" level and to equalize returns across different uses of resources. Ricardo writes:

> 'In speaking then, of commodities, of their exchangeable value, and of the laws which regulate their relative prices, we mean always such commodities .... on the production of which competition operates without restraint.' [1]

And from John Stuart Mill:

> 'So far as rents profits, wages, prices, are determined by competition, laws may be assigned for them. Assume competition to be

their exclusive regulator and principles of broad generality and scientific precision may be laid down, according to which they will be regulated.'

Yet several economists, some quite prominent, consider perfect competition a woefully inadequate model of competitive activity.[2]   Those dissatisfied with the model of perfect competition make several related points, but chief among these are that it gives excessive attention to only one kind of competition, price competition, and that perfect competition is too static to reflect the essence of competitive activity. An example may be given from a frequently quoted passage by Joseph Schumpeter

> '.....it is not that kind of competition which counts but the competition from the new commodity, the new technology, the new source of supply, the new type of organization ..... competition which commands a decisive cost or quality advantage and which strikes not at the margin of the profits and the outputs of the existing firms but at their foundations and their very lives. This kind of competition is so much more effective than the other as a bombardment is in comparison with forcing a door, and so much more important that it becomes a matter of comparative indifference whether competition in the ordinary sense functions more or less promptly.' [3]

Not only are there many dimensions to Schumpeter's process of "creative destruction," but included among them is the attempt to acquire and to maintain monopoly.

Hayek notes in *Individualism and Economic Order* that the idea of perfect competition

> '.....assumes that state of affairs already to exist which ..... the process of competition tends to bring about .....(I)f the state of affairs assumed by the theory of perfect competition ever existed, it would not only deprive of their scope all the activities which the verb 'to compete' describes but would make them virtually impossible.' [4]

Joan Robinson would not take a much different position about perfect competition.

These criticisms are not based on the notion that elements of monopoly permeate the economy, such as is Chamberlin's *Theory of Monopolistic Competition*. They complain that the economic concept of competition fails to reflect what these critics see as the essence of competition, that it neglects the dynamics of competitive activity, ignores the importance of time to competitive processes, and treats superficially the motivation for competitive activity. The puzzle in the economic notion of competition is that although competition plays an indispensable role in the analysis of economic

systems, its only formal treatment, the perfect
competition model, seems seriously defective. [5]

Many critics, especially among Austrian
economists, are more comfortable with the treatment
accorded competition by the classical economists
than with the more recent emphasis on the necessary
and sufficient conditions for competition to yield an
optimal allocation of resources. A review of the
treatment of competition by classical writers,
however, would reveal only vague and loose
statements, not definitve analyses or careful
modeling. The very casualness of their discussions of
competition provides a useful clue as to the source of
our difficulty with competition. After all, men the
likes of Smith, Ricardo, and Mill, if they had put
their minds to it, could have written insightful,
perhaps brilliant, discussions of competition. That
they did not indicates their objective was elsewhere.
They took competition for granted, assuming it to be
a pervasive restraint on the pursuit of self-interest.
They relied on it to move resources out of tasks
yielding lower rates of return and into tasks yielding
higher returns. But they showed no deep interest in
analyzing competition itself.

The problem central to their interests was mastery
of the nature and consequences of *decentralization.*
They assumed competition would pervasively guide
decentralized activity, but what they sought was an
understanding of how the parts of a complex
economic system were related to each other and to

the whole. The phenomenon on which they focused was the price system, for they realized that prices provided the linkage between decentralized activities. Whereas competition is with us always and is always important, decentralization and the price system achieved a new significance during their time. During the better part of the period in which the neo-classicists wrote, the 19th Century, strong central governments gave way to individual private actions in an unprecendented move toward freedom. The economies of Western societies became increasingly decentralized, relying on the price system to a degree never experienced before. The price system, quite understandably, is what attracted the attention and fired the imagination of economists. If the perfect competition model is seen as a tool for understanding the price system, and not for understanding competition, it represents a natural evolution from, and vital capstone to, the central interests of the classical writers. Part of the difficulties with competition come from our attempt to use the perect competition model for a purpose for which it is not ideally suited - for analyzing competitive *activity*.

However, the perfect competition model, or something much like it, is required to understand the functioning of the price system in a decentralized economy. A bewildering menu of facts and observations is offered by the hustle and bustle of the marketplace and the institutions embedded in it. Making sense of these required a model   with considerable abstraction and generalization. Although Smith's work is rich in institutional description, its real strength lies in his ability to generalize the motivation of self-interest across different activities and institutions. He was able to see that these interests are disciplined by each other and that they are linked sensibly through prices. Abstraction and refinement intensified. Ricardo's writings give little attention to institutional detail. This trend continued as more highly polished and finely tuned abstract models of the price system were produced by mainstream economists during the 100 years following Smith, culminating in Walra's general equilibrium model.

Abstraction from *all* real world phenomena, however, would have led to pure mathematics. An artful choice between phenomena to be explained and phenomena to be abstracted from, depending on the objective of the inquiry, was required. The neo-classical inquiry into decentralization retained the price system for study, setting aside considerations of the underlying system of law, government, and also the various sources of economic "friction" so central to Schumpeterian and Hayekian notions of competition. Firms and households increasingly represented mere calculating machines whose inner workings were of little interest. Markets became empirically empty conceptualizations of the forums in which exchange costlessly took place. The legal system and the government were relegated to the distant background by the simple device of stating, without clarification, that resources were "privately owned." *Laissez faire* was more than policy; to the evolving discipline of economics, it was a methodologically convenient way of specializing the problem being studied to that of a "pure" price system, unencumbered by political considerations. These "details", so important in any real economic system were either taken as exogenous, converted to pure formalism, or simply ignored.

And appropriately so. The coordinating functions of the price system are more easily revealed by concentrating attention on the operation of such a system under long-run conditions, conditions for which these "details" really are details. The perfect competition model is the intellectual tool for conceptualizing such conditions. It is the price system the model explicates, not competitive activity. Competitive *activity* itself is difficult to comprehend through a model that assumes away transaction and information costs.

The partial abstraction actually arrived at was hardly anticipated or planned, but it did greatly improve our understanding of the coordinating function of the price system. The model that finally emerged presented a thorough, consistent, and brilliant conceptualization of the role of prices in linking decentralized activities. All in all, the result still dazzles, the simplification of complexity still impresses.

The considerable attention given to the price system, however, led to the neglect not only of those "details", but, surprisingly, to some aspects of decentralization also. It was not until much later that Hayek saw in decentralization a method for efficiently using knowledge of particular conditions, knowledge not known as well to all as to those familiar with the situation. The full information assumptions of the perfect competition model clearly delayed recognition of this important aspect of decentralization. It also encouraged the neglect of those islands of authority, firms and households, which, by exercising limited authority in a sea of prices, could translate such special knowledge into goods and services.

The power of the perfect competition model rests on a remarkable conceptualization of an important limiting case of the coordination problem - *the complete absence of conscious control by anyone over the plans of others*. Government authority is kept to the background by the assumption of *laissez-faire*. The formalization of institutions does the same for firms and households. The coordinating function of the price system is thus isolated and highlighted by imagining it to operate in a perfectly decentralized setting in which no element of authority is present. The formulation of perfect decentralization *is* the accomplishment of the perfect competition model. Indeed, it is more properly named the *perfect decentralization model*. And so I rechristen it for the purpose of these lectures. The model adds much to our understanding of coordination through price, nothing to our understanding of coordination through authority,and only little to our understanding of competitive *actions*.

The complete absence of authority is formally achieved by making price-takers of all decision-makers and by determining prices only through the aggregate impact of large numbers of independently reached individual decisions.   Since all decision-makers have knowledge of all prices and production processes, they are barred from possessing that specialized knowledge to which Hayek refers when he defends decentralization. Time plays no real role in the model, so risk taking behavior, especially that which involves the commitment of investments to specialized assets, is negelcted. Firms and households function only as calculating machines that errorlessly put maximizing solutions into the price/quantity matrix. In completely decentralized markets, prices and knowledge offer no instrument through which one decision-maker's actions can be controlled or bested by another's.   The model stands on assumptions guaranteed to bar any conscious interdependence of decision making.   Unlike the athletic arena where both the outcome of the contest and the manner in which it is played turn on the real time behavior of an individual seeking to influence or to best others, perfect decentralization deprives a participant in the marketplace of any impact on prices, total quantities produced, or actions of others. The actors and institutions might just as well be on separate planets, each actor responding only through quantity adjustments to prices telegraphed to him by that great impersonal price-maker, the Market. The assumed absence of both "friction" and ignorance cuts through a maze of detail and brings the analysis to a stable resting point within a framework in which personal interaction plays no role and authority is absent, but in which, nonetheless, there is functional interdependence.   It is a grand intellectual achievement, the only theory yet devised that is capable of imparting an understanding of how the price system integrates decentralized economic decisions.[6]

The quickness and depth of the insights it provides have been purchased at a price, however. It seriously slights the legal and political setting in which decentralization functions in a real capitalistic system (a subject to be discussed in the next lecture), and it also neglects the importance to competitive processes of time, uncertainty, and the cost of transacting. These are sacrified to the cause of determining how the "natural" prices of long-run equilibrium integrate decentralized economic decisions; these natural prices presumably are unaffected by time, uncertainty, and the "frictions" of the short-run. This is accomplished by developing a very special notion of competition - call it perfect price competition.   Perfect price competition, the instantaneous and complete adjustment of price to marginal cost, admirably accomplished the objective of understanding how the price system integrates decentralized decisions. Nor can there be much real doubt that the competition of a real *laissez-faire* economic system would move short-run prices toward those that have the properties exhibited by the equilibrium prices of perfect price competition.

The special notion of competition relied upon by the perfect decentralization model makes that model a poor vehicle for understanding a wide variety of competitive tactics and institutions that are adopted precisely to accommodate to time, uncertainty, and the cost of transacting. Particular marketing practices, such as tie-in sales, reciprocity, and manufacturer control of the prices at which retailers resell their goods are difficult to explain with a model that assumes away their cause. Vertical integration and the very existence of firms find little rationale in the perfect decentralization model because their source lies in the uncertainties of real economic systems and in the cost of using markets to accommodate to these uncertainties.

If perfect price competition is inadequate to the task of explaining particular pricing practices and economic institutions, it is nonetheless quite potent in assessing economic consequences in situations for which such tactics and institutions are unimportant. Exogenous developments, assumed to be beyond the

control of individuals and their institutions, are
readily analyzed to yield predictable consequences as
a result of competition.

An analogy from botany is useful. As a tree grows
and its foliage becomes denser, the shadow it casts
grows darker and larger. The grasses that grow at the
tree's base compete for the decreasing amount of sun,
although I think they do so quite impersonally. The
population of grasses necessarily changes its composi-
tion to one that favors varieties better able to
function with less sun. Similar changes are wrought
in economic systems by an alteration in the
exogenous circumstances governing the varieties of
economic products and processes. Assume an
exogenous change in the pattern of demand. Dollars
fall like sunshine upon some industries but not
others. The former grow, the latter decline, and
personal action hardly can alter the allocative impact
of this change in the pattern of demand.

Most competitive adjustments are admixtures of
such passive adaptation and active competition, but
the perfect decentralization model, poorly equipped
by its assumptions to help us understand active
competition, is more helpful in regard to passive
adaptation. The exogenous imposition of a tax, a
tariff, or a technological change leads to resource
reallocations that are quite well understood through
the use of the perfect decentralization mode. No
substantial analysis of active competition is needed to
deduce that a domestic industry protected by a tariff

will be larger than if not protected, or that the same industry measured worldwide will be smaller, or that the gains to the domestic industry are more than offset by the losses to its customers. The perfect decentralization model very much facilitates an intelligent appraisal of the impact of such policies.

But, just as active competition and passive adaptation are seldom completely independent of each other, so some awkwardness arises when the perfect decentralization model is used to explain how exogenous developments shift the equilibrium allocation of resources. It turns out to be desirable to use at least a modicum of active competition, in the form of price setting behavior, in such an explanation, even though this is strictly inconsistent with the model's assumptions. A typical exposition of such a change might proceed as follows. An exogenous increase in demand causes a shortage at the initial equilibrium price, and the equilibrium price adjusts to eliminate the shortage. But if all market participants are price-takers, why should the shortage and the initial price not persist? One way to motivate participants to alter their behavior is to let them abandon the price-taker role in favor of price-maker. For a good in short supply, buyers are suddenly allowed to *compete* actively by offering higher prices in an attempt to move to the front of the queue. For a good in excess supply, sellers are suddenly allowed to *compete* actively by asking lower prices in the attempt to sell their supplies before

other sellers. Such competitive activity makes sense
only if frictions of one sort or another bar
instantaneous imitation. To move the model from
one equilibrium to another, it is convenient to break
out of the frictionless price-taker behavior model and
introduce an unexplained dose of friction that sets
rivalrous behavior into motion.

II.   The Consideration Of Monopoly

The general lack of concern about monopoly in
classical and neoclassical writings is evidence of the
specialized search by these economists for an understanding of the co-ordinating role of prices in
long-run equilibrium   If the frictions and ignorance
of the short-run were of no interest to them in this
search, then certainly monopoly, which has all the
earmarks of a short-run phenomenon, could hardly
provoke their interest. Their faith in competition did
not allow these authors to consider monopoly a
serious problem in the formal solution to the economizing problem.   At most, it was a temporary
problem occasioned by wrongheaded public policies
that barred competition.   Although Smith observed
that:

> 'People of the same trade seldom convene
> without their entertainment ending in a con-
> spiracy against the public or a scheme for an
> increase in price.', [7]

his fears about monopoly were very much directed to government protection. The subject of monopoly essentially remains outside his analysis, a tradition characterizing much of economic analysis until the decade of the 1930's.

Smith's and Ricardo's attempts to relate price to cost of production or to a labor theory of value offer no comfortable place for monopoly since monopoly opens a wedge between price and cost. They simply brushed aside monopoly when discussing the consequences of decentralization. Indeed the formal theory of monopoly (to be distinguished from casual discussion) did not enter economics until 1838 when Cournot derived the formal marginal revenue = marginal cost monopoly equilibrium.

A casual survey of the importance of monopoly in classical economic thought seems appropriate. A tabulation of the number of index citations to pages discussing monopoly reveals that, in the main, it hardly attracted interest.

1.   Adam Smith, 10 pages of 903
          (The Wealth of Nations)

2.   David Ricardo, 5 pages of 292
          (Political Economy of Taxation)

3.   John S. Mill, 2 pages of 1,004
          (Principles of Political Economy).

Surely, there is more discussion under different

titles than this survey indicates. Some discussions of government policy probably should be included, but the fact is that the classical economists were much more concerned about fixed supplies of land than about monopoly, and a careful study would reveal this. Even Marx and his followers failed to attach much importance to monopoly. Their view of the functioning of society in the large was clearly based on competition, albeit competition between classes rather than between firms. The only really significant role accorded to monopoly by older Marxist writings was in the asserted exploitation of underdeveloped countries by government protected monopolies.

The fact is that the most important theme of the period was the necessity of competition. The ideas of Malthus, Smith, Darwin, and Huxley dominated the intellectual scene with their emphasis on competition. Try as one may, no counter-part to the economic concept of monopoly can be found in the socio-biological scheme of things. In that context, monopoly must be viewed merely as a particular outcome of competition. And, at least as late as 1900, economists as a whole shared this belief.

Some insights into the professional view of American economists can be had in the pronouncements of those who were active in the foundation of the American Economic Association just prior to the turn of the century. (This sample is weighted heavily by those who had socialist leanings.) They did not view relatively small firm size as necessarily desirable, but as a form of organization that was sometimes beneficial and sometimes not. It did not strike them as difficult to justify industrial concentration. They were swept along by the tide of Darwinian thought. Combinations and trusts were regarded as evolutionary social advances, as the outcome of natural laws calling for social cooperation to replace personal actions. They also felt such combinations reflected technological changes calling for larger scale operations. This view was held by John Bates Clark, a person not obviously overwhelmed by Darwinism but one who excelled in his profession. He wrote:

> 'Combinations have their roots in the nature of social industry and are normal in their origin, their development, and their practical working. They are neither to be depressed by scientists nor suppressed by legislators. They are the result of an evolution, and are the happy outcome of a competition so abnormal that the continuance of it would have meant widespread ruin. A successful attempt to suppress them by law would involve the reversion of industrial systems to a cast-off type, the renewal of abuses from which society has escaped by a step in development.' [8]

Senior and Mill expressed the same belief much earlier, as did many English and German economists. Most vocal economists of Clark's day felt not only that the government ***ought*** not interfere with such organizational evolution, but, perhaps more important, that no act of law ***could*** interfere with the natural progress of institutions. There surely existed contrary views, but they were not voiced loudly by many economists when the American Economic Association was formed. This professional opinion carried its usual zero weight in Congress where American political populism assured the passage, in 1890, of the Sherman Antitrust Act. The United States is now almost two centuries into its unique experiment to strengthen economic competition (however silly that may seem to sociobiologists). The prominent role, played by the perfect decentralization model in this experiment merits later comment.

III. *Multidimensional Competition*

Market processes work neither instantaneously nor with full knowledge, so perfect price competition hardly exhausts the many ways in which self-interest is pursued. Competing through product quality, contractual arrangements, and institutional innovation, and through tactical quickness and alertness, all become meaningful. Beyond these economic channels of competition there are the courts and governments, and in these also will be found the competitive pursuit of self-interest. This competition will manifest itself in ways and in facts that are difficult to comprehend through the perfect decentralization model.

Economists in recent years have been examining some of these additional dimensions of competition. American economists have been forced to face up to the many facets of market competition because of their growing involvement in the American antitrust experiment. Antitrust cases often involve business practices difficult to understand in terms of either the perfect price competition or monopoly models. In addition, the growing involvement of governments in their economies could not be ignored by economists after the decade of the 1930's. During the 19th Century, the outlet for the bulk of competitive activity was found in the private sector, but this became distinctly less so after World War II. The *laissez-faire* economy, a convenient tool for focusing attention on the once clearly dominant decentralized private sector, is hardly a convenient framework for studying competitive activity during the 20th Century.

In response to these social developments, and also to the desire to push beyond the recent limits of our understanding, a revolution in the focus of economic work has been taking place during the last three decades. The new interests of economists increasingly center on the very matters abstracted from by our professional predecessors. The focus is on the economics of information and transactions, and the context for the investigation of these has enlarged to include legal and political institutions.

FOOTNOTES

[1] David Ricardo, **The Principles of Political Economy and Taxation** (London: J.M. Dent, 1955), p.6.

[2] An excellent expression of this dissatisfaction may be found in McNulty, Paul J., "Economic Theory and the Meaning of Competition" **Quarterly Journal of Economics**, Vol. 82, (1968).

[3] Joseph Schumpeter, **Capitalism, Socialism, and Democracy**, (New York: Harper and Row, 1962), p. 84.

[4] F.A. Hayek, **Individualism and Economic Order** (Chicago: University of Chicago Press, 1948), pp. 92-6.

[5] See G.J. Stigler, "Perfect Competition, Historically Contemplated," **Journal of Political Economy**, Feb. 1957, for a distinction between perfect markets and perfect competition that addresses some of these puzzles.

[6] More modern treatments of the perfect competition model attempt to integrate time and uncertainty into price taker behavior. The "state preference" approach articulated by Kenneth Arrow and Gerard Debreu dates and attaches probabilities to all possible states of affair. General equilibrium conditions are derived on the basis of price-taker behavior, yielding a modern extension of the perfect competition model. Competitive activity, however, derives from the impossibility of a complete set of all probability states. The modern extension does not much facilitate our understanding of how persons competitively seek the advantage of timing and better knowledge.

[7] Adam Smith, **The Wealth of Nations.**

[8] J.M. Clark, "The Limits of Competition," reprinted in Clark and Giddings, **The Modern Distributive Process** (1888).

Lecture 2

COMPETITION IN THE PRIVATE SECTOR

I.   Introduction

This lecture begins by developing the implications of competition when information and transaction costs are too important to ignore. The assumptions of the perfect decentralization model are thus breeched, and the framework for economizing becomes much more like that of a *laissez-faire* society. Brief consideration is then given to the court system, which may be thought of as the legal underpinning of a *laissez-faire* society, and to antitrust policy, which, although it strains the *laissez-faire* framework, is nonetheless designed in principle to support competition in the private sector. Competition in the public sector is discussed in the third lecture.

II.   Laissez-faire Competition

The *laissez-faire* economy brings the conditions of competition into close approximation to those to which the perfect decentralization model seems to pertain. The legal substructure is private; the use of payments to influence the behavior of others is neither prohibited nor frowned upon. But the 'frictions" that perfect decentralization assumes away, must be lived with in *laissez-faire*. Of these "frictions", the most important are those that derive from positive information and transaction costs. *Laissez-faire* competition, reacting to these costs, reveals itself in ways not readily understood through the perfect decentralization model. Before considering these manifestations of competition, let us reconsider the function of competition in a *laissez-faire* economy, as this function is understood by mainstream economists.

III. The Filtering Function of 'Laissez-faire'

Competition in a private property system is expected to guide resources to those uses that maximize the value of production secured from them. This value is measured by what consumers are willing to pay, making due allowance for the implicit value of leisure and other goods consumed outside the formal market arena. The profit criterion stops uses of resources that would result in more cost than benefit as these are measured by the money votes of consumers. Harmful effects are possible, but only when they are outweighed by beneficial effects. Thus, if the new product is to succeed, the harmful effects imposed of producers of related old products must be more than offset by the combined gains of consumers and the product innovator. If these benefits do not outweigh the costs of innovation, the innovator's rivals will be able and willing to reduce the prices of their products sufficiently to defeat the new product. New products and activities succeed only when they result in a net gain in the total value of what is produced.

Two characteristics of the *laissez-faire* setting are relevant to the workability of this filtering mechanism. First, because the filtering is done according to willingness to pay, not according to some theoretical index of global utility maximization, *laissez-faire* offers an easily measured money unit guide to resource movement. Secondly, because ownership is private, persons are motivated by their own wealth considerations to respond to this guide. To the extent that the consequences of competition in the private sector are approximated by deductions from the perfect decentralization model, the filter provided by *laissez-faire* satisfies certain well-known equilibrium conditions. These are summarized by the conclusion that competition allocates resources so that the value of output, from the perspective of consumers, is maximized; competition also distributes income through prices and wages that equal the marginal productivity of the inputs used to create this value.

This view of competition in the private sector certainly has not won universal endorsement. One major set of critiques is to be found in Marxian views of surplus value and expropriation of the product of labor. Another critique, more germane to my subject, is characterized by the writings of Oscar

Lange and Abba Lerner. This critique objects to the distributive consequences of *laissez-faire* competition while still favoring the productive efficiency it achieves. The remedy proposed seeks to instruct socialist managers to respond to prices much as would their capitalist counterparts, but instructs a socialist government to distribute the wealth thereby produced in more egalitarian fashion than would *laissez-faire* competition. This program completely fails to recognize the essential linkage between the efficiency with which output is produced and the private property base that motivates behavior. Competition in the private property system brings to bear on an owner of resources, including human capital, the consequences of his use of these resources precisely because he is their owner. His wealth position is directly affected by how well he fares with consumers. The threat of suffering a loss in the value of what *he owns* is what causes him to remain loyal to the sovereignty of consumers. Separate his actions from this discipline, by shifting the wealth consequences of his behavior to the socialist state, and his motivation to serve consumers is weakened. Lange and Lerner offer no practical substitute source of motivation. Nor do they consider the very real problem of motivating government to abide by their egalitarian principle.

For mainstream economists, there remains the important question of the applicability to *laissez-faire* of conclusions drawn from perfect decentralization, a model that assumes away authority, monopoly, externalities, and ignorance. I turn now to a consideration of these problems.

IV. The Functions of Control

The perfect decentralization model leaves no room for the exercise of authority or of control, and, in particular, it provides no rationale for the firm, which is the focus of control in a *laissez-faire* economy. This difficulty was recognized by R.H. Coase in his famous article on "The Nature of the Firm". [1] Coase relies on transaction cost to explain the existence of firms. Were markets costless to use, there would be no need to give up the flexibility and independence of exchange when cooperation with others is advantageous. The greater the cost of transacting, the more difficult it is to arrange and consummate such exchanges. The comparative advantage of organizing such cooperation on the basis of *authority* within business firms thus increases with transaction cost. Business firms, in which controlled cooperation takes place, are the first important implication of costly transactions.

The *laissez-faire* filtering process, using the profit test, selects some of these business organizations for survival and rejects others. In our article on the theory of the firm, [2] Professor Alchian and I argue that effectively accommodating to the problem of shirking is important in meeting this test of survival.

The shirking problem arises because informational costs raise barriers to ascertaining each member's contribution to a firm's output. Merely valuing the firm's output does not permit easy assignment of individual marginal productivities to members of the firm's team   This would be no problem if there were no gains to cooperating through a team effort, for then each member could produce for market his separate contribution to the final product. In that case, his productivity could be measured more easily through market transactions. When team production is efficient, however, each owner of a cooperating input has an incentive to under-utilize his resources. The gain from doing so accrues only to him. The cost is imposed on the entire team.

The team, and each of its members, is desirous of reducing shirking, and this will be done if the cost of reducing shirking is less than the cost of shirking itself. The increase in marketable output that would result allows all team members to substitute higher take-home income for the very specific nonpecuniary consumption provided by shirking. All that is needed are appropriate methods for directing and monitoring the cooperative effort.

If information and exchange costs were negligible, market exchanges between the individual team members could reduce the shirking. Each owner of a resource could receive revenues proportional to the value of what *he* actually produces. Because information and exchange costs are positive and team

production is productive, the organization of the firm
will affect its ability to cope with the internal
shirking problem.   Authoritative control, by
agreement with team members, becomes productive.
Duties are assigned, performance is monitored by
management; shirking by workmen is thereby
reduced. Shirking by those who manage is reduced
by tying managerial income in greater degree to the
market determined value of what is produced by the
team, thus, to an extent, reintroducing the market
filter.

   The internal organization of what might be called
the "classical" firm, headed by an owner-manager,
whose income is correlated with the market
determined value of his firm's output, but manned by
the stereotype of directed factory workers, emerges
as an efficient form of team cooperation under
certain conditions. These are characterized by owner
supplied capital and by directability of the labor
force in carrying out its tasks. If capital can be raised
at lower cost by acquiring smaller amounts of it from
a variety of sources, the corporate organization,
comprised of many shareholders, acquires survival
characteristics, even though managerial shirking may
increase somewhat. If the tasks of the labor force are
not so easily directed, and if the number of team
members is small, firms comprised of active partners,
such as characterize the legal and medical professions,
can survive the filter of the profit test.   In such
partnerships, profit sharing substitutes for the

managing of inputs in creating incentives to reduce
shirking, but since shirking then becomes a shared
cost borne by the entire team there remains some
pressure for partner to monitor partner and to make
profit shares at least partly responsive to some
indexes of work load.

Since the problem of ascertaining behavior also
characterizes exchange across markets, "pseudo"
firms will evolve to supplement market transactions.
The cooperating inputs susceptible to shirking need
not all work for the same firm. I refer here primarily
to relationships between buyers and sellers who,
while retaining their separate identities, find it
desirable to convey control over some of their
internal operations to the other party to the
exchange. Some aspects of a vertically integrated
firm are melded into a market transaction, an
arrangement for which there would be no rationale in
the perfect decentralization model. The function of
such an agreement is to reduce shirking by parties
external to the firm.

An illustration is provided in Judge William
Howard Taft's discussion of the Pullman case in the
opinion he wrote for the Addyston Pipe and Steel
Case, a famous early American antitrust case. The
Pullman Company had agreed to supply and service
railroad sleeping cars to a purchasing railroad, but
only on the condition that the railroad would not do
business with any other sleeping car company on the
same line to which the cars and service were to be

supplied. The railroad agreed to this constraint on its managerial discretion, but later sought to avoid it by alleging that antitrust law prohibited such restraints on its business decisions. Judge Taft's opinion of the contract follows:

> The main purpose of such a contract is to furnish sleeping-car facilities to the public. The railroad company may discharge this duty itself to the public, and allow no one else to do it, or it may hire someone to do it, and, to secure the necessary investment of capital in the discharge of the duty, may secure to the sleeping-car company the same freedom from competition that it would have itself in discharging the duty. The restraint upon itself is properly proportioned to, and is only ancillary to, the main purpose of the contract, which is to secure proper facilities to the public.

We may ask why such a guarantee of exclusive rights to serve the railroad was required to induce the requisite investment of capital by the Pullman Company? The answer surely is that the usefulness of the investment was limited to servicing the particular needs of the railroad, either because such orders for sleeping cars were not frequent or because the specifications were rather unique. If the railroad should turn later to other suppliers, Pullman's investments would suffer a loss in value. A possibility for opportunistic behavior, or shirking, by the railroad therefore exists. The railroad, after Pullman's investment, and in the absence of a contracted restriction on its behavior, might demand that the price of the ordered sleeping cars be lowered under threat of turning to another supplier.

The source of shirking is in the high cost of forecasting future behavior in situations where low cost production requires a precommitment of highly specific and durable investments by one or both parties to an exchange. The contractual arrangement is readily explained as the result of competitive activity to secure railroad services efficiently when uncertainty and time play important roles in the production process. Such an arrangement is not readily understood by applying the perfect decentralization model. That model's assumptions offer no rationale for assigning importance to uncertainty and time. Nor do modern extensions of that model, such as the Arrow-Debreu preference state analysis, cope well with this uncertainty problem. The usual assumption in these extensions is that all contingencies can be anticipated and that their probabilities are known. This assumption denies the importance of transaction cost and of the uncertainty with which these probabilistic expectations are held, both of which are the root causes of the exchange problem.

The problem might be resolved through contractual restrictions of the sort just described, or it might be resolved through outright merger of the two firms. The option of vertical integration through merger [3] is more likely to be chosen if the desired cooperation is long-run and important. When it is not, the restrictive contractual agreement is the preferred route because it retains the advantages of specialization monitored by markets. Enlarging the firm increases the severity of the internal shirking problem.

Often the contractual restrictions required to resolve external shirking problems involve the control by a manufacturer of the price at which a retailer offers to resell the manufacturer's good to consumers. When manufacturers desire to have various services provided at the point of sale, a way must be devised to reduce the retailer's incentives to "free ride" on the provision of services by other retailers. [4] The manufacturer of appliances, for example, may find it in his interest, and in the consumer's interest, to have displayed and explained a wide variety of models of his product line. Only some of these models will be big sellers. A nearby discount retailer may offer only these, thus reducing his inventory and sales costs, relying on the full-line store to supply consumers the information and comparisons they desire. After consumers receive such service from the full-line store, whose prices must cover the cost of the service provided, they then purchase the desired item at a lower price in the nearby discount store. The end result of this opportunistic behavior is to make it unprofitable for retailers to supply the efficient amount of retail services.

One way to reduce the severity of the problem is for the manufacturer to require that all retailers resell at a price sufficiently high to cover the cost of providing the desired services, thus undermining the consumer's incentive to shop in a full-line store but buy in a discount store that does not provide the desired service. The entire problem fails to appear in the perfect decentralization model because that model assumes consumers are fullly informed about products and prices.

The particular mix of contractual restrictions and vertical integration used to solve these problems will vary according to the specific conditions of each case. Solutions surviving the test of competition in a *laissez-faire* setting are those that best meet the demands of consumers. Completely separated firms, cooperating entirely through market transactions, characterize one important extreme on this continuum. A variety of contractual restrictions occupy the middle of the continuum; at the other extreme, lies full vertical integration. This variety of structural solutions arises in response to the specific information and transaction problems associated with coordination of productive efforts.

V.   *The Size Distribution of Firms*

Rising marginal cost limits the size of what passes

for a firm in the perfect decentralization model, and the resulting atomistic structure of industry makes price - taker behavior a reasonable expectation. A sufficient, but not necessary condition for markets in a *laissez-faire* economy to be concentrated is significant scale economies. *Laissez-faire* competition selects those industry structures compatible with underlying cost conditions. This would be the only reason for markets to be concentrated under *laissez-faire* competition if the other assumptions of perfect decentralization fit the actual conditions of competition. But they do not.

Information is not costless, so that all prospective competitors cannot know all production techniques and profit opportunities. Information cost refers not just to the cost ascertaining how successful firms have prospered, but also of reliably judging whether the same formula for success *will continue* into the future. Some firms will enter *first* or will perform *better*, not only in discovering new production techniques, but in anticipating consumer demands. For some period of time, these firms will remain relatively large in their industires even if their large production rates bring operations to where marginal cost increases.

If the conditions of competition in some industries combine costly information and a general absence of sharply rising marginal production cost, then there is every reason to expect that *laissez-faire* competition will lead to skewed industry structures.

A uniform size distribution of firms would fail to reflect the real comparative efficiencies of specific firms, as these efficiencies emerge over time. The skewed structure of industry should be correlated with a similar skewness in the structure of accounting profit rates. The larger, more successful firms should record higher profit rates.[5] Successful technological breakthroughs, whose impacts are not restrained by rapidly rising marginal costs, can be expected simultaneously to increase market share and profit for the larger, more successful firms, because positive information cost makes such success difficult to imitate. Table 1, reporting correlations between profit rates and industry concentration for U.S. manufacturing firms, is consistent with this expectation. For large firms, there is a positive correlation between profit rate and the concentration of the industry they occupy. This correlation is not present for small and medium sized firms. This is inconsistent with a *simple* collusion explanation. Successful collusion in concentrated industries would raise the profit rates of all firms in the industry, not just the larger firms. Whether these data derive from *laissez-faire* competition in a setting in which information cost is significant or from more successful collusion in more concentrated industries, it must be the case that larger firms in concentrated industries have lower costs or better products. Such differences in performance do not themselves reflect collusion, but fundamentally derive from competitive

TABLE 1

SIMPLE CORRELATIONS BETWEEN RATE OF RETURN AND CONCENTRATION BY ASSET SIZE OF FIRMS[1]

Asset Size ($000)	Year				
	1958	1963	1966	1967	1970
$0–500	−.09	−.19 [b]	−.09	−.01	−.38 [a]
500–5,000	.08	−.00	−.06	−.07	−.01
5,000–50,000	.16	.11	.04	−.05	−.00
50,000–100,000	−.06	.01	.09	.10	−.03
100,000 and up	−.00	.16	.16	.16	.28 [b]
$0 and up	.29 [a]	.35 [a]	.28 [a]	.19 [b]	.27 [b]

Source: See Harold Demsetz, Two Systems of Belief About Monopoly, in **Industrial Concentration: The New Learning,** Tab. 8 at 178 (Columbia Law School Conference on Industrial Concentration, Airlie House, Harvey J. Goldschmid et al., 1974).

[1] Concentration is based on four-digit U.S. Census industries weighted by employment to match the Internal Revenue Service data on pretax profit and interest used to calculate rates of return on total assets.

[a] Significant at 1 per cent level.

[b] Significant at 5 per cent level.

rivalry in a milieu of positive information cost. But, even should these data reflect monopoly, it is, in a real sense, the choice of consumers who could avoid monopoly were they more willing to absorb the information and other costs of turning quickly to new rivals.

VI.   *Fraud and Deception*

The degree of vertical integration and the relative size of a firm in any given product market are ways in which *laissez-faire* competition adjusts to the fact of positive information cost.   Many informational problems are not resolved by such structural adjustments, but instead give rise to the exchange of information itself between those who will cooperate across markets.   The importance of mass communication in developed economies, often in the form of commercial advertising, reflects the large demand for information.   This demand is especially great in economies in which economic activities are highly specialized, the productivity of communication surely being greater where specialists interact across markets than where self-sufficiency abounds.   It is not surprising that the fraction of GNP devoted to mass communication is higher in developed economies than in undeveloped.   That basic economic forces are at work is reflected in the high correlation across developed economies of the intensity with which a specific industry advertises.

Unfortunately, specialization within an economy not only increases productivity, but, when information is costly, it also creates opportunities for dishonest dealings. It will often be true that the quality of what is to be exchanged is difficult to ascertain before the transaction is concluded. Goods and services, and the checks written to pay for them, may not be of the expected quality. Specialization, or the productivity of specialization, encourages reliance on persons whose interests are not usually identical. Although the courts are available in a *laissez-faire* economy to help realize exchange expectations it would be uneconomic for any type of society to attempt to eliminate all dishonest dealings. Competition in a *laissez-faire* setting, however, does bring forth techniques and behavior that attenuate the problem. Obvious among these are the offer of a wide variety of guarantees including "money back if dissatisfied." These are presumably enforceable, at some cost, in the courts of a *laissez-faire* economy. In addition, there is the offer of third party guarantees, for a fee of course. For example, the use of a VISA charge plate insures a merchant against the buyer's failure to pay.

What is it that makes most of these guarantees believable ? And why, in fact, are they quite generally honored by the guarantors A good part of the answer, if not all, surely lies in the fact that dishonest behavior in private property system often would impose more cost than gain on the dishonest party. Owners of firms (and of reputations) suffer a loss in the market values of their entitlement once it is know that they deal dishonestly. Dishonest dealing increases the expected difficulty in securing revenues in the future. Costs will need to be borne to restore tarnished reputations or to lower prices sufficiently to reestablish trade.

The expected loss in future revenue because of dishonest dealings is not independent of circumstances.[6] A firm that looks forward to a large sales volume and/or enjoys high profit margins has more to loose than a firm that is likely to remain small or that realizes only small profit margins. Relatively large firms receiving relatively high profit margins, therefore, will tend to be more reliable trading partners. The well known consumer habit of associating price with quality and reliability is not foolish when information is costly. Firms whose investments are very specific to the market in which they operate are less likely to behave dishonestly because they cannot easily sell or use their assets for other goods should these assets lose value in serving the market for which they were created. A prior investment in advertising a product, for example, builds an intangible asset whose value is largely tied to the brand being advertised. A history of specific investment in brand advertising therefore reduces the likelihood of dishonest behavior. Again, consumers are not foolish for believing that highly advertised brands are more reliable. At the other extreme are

UNIVERSITY OF WINNIPEG
LIBRARY
515 Portage Avenue
Winnipeg, Manitoba R3B 2E9

small retail establishments in markets with high customer turnover, such as those serving tourists. The expected loss in future revenue is considerably smaller relative to the short-run gains, to both sellers and buyers, from behaving dishonestly in such situations, and we may expect to encounter opportunistic behavior more frequently in such situations.

Persons are defended against fraud not only by their own astuteness, or by the courts to which they may appeal, defenses that require some sophistication, but also by competition, a protection that may aid even the naive and innocent. Consider a packer of coffee that puts a bit less than one pound of coffee into a one pound can. He stands to profit from his dishonesty as long as he can sell that can at the going price for one pound of coffee. Consumers may have no great incentive to police a situation in which they overpay, say, only .05 percent, so this firm's practice may continue to be unnoticed by consumers. However, other coffee packers have an interest in discovering why this packer seems to be prospering. They have an incentive to measure the contents of his coffee cans. After discovering his dishonesty, they may bring it to the attention of the consumers, in which case they obviously benefit, or they may behave dishonestly themselves, in which case it is not so obvious how competition comes to the consumer's aid. But it does. The marginal cost of supplying cans that are only partly filled with

UNIVERSITY OF WINNIPEG
LIBRARY
515 Portage Avenue
Winnipeg, Manitoba R3B 2E9

coffee is less than that of supplying full cans, so the number of such cans supplied to the market must increase because of this competitive dishonesty. The price of the can of coffee will fall under this competitive pressure until the consumer again pays approximately the same price per pound of coffee as if honest measure had been given. It might be thought that the fraud will simply be repeated again, reducing by another increment the amount of coffee in a one pound can. But ultimately the quantity of coffee becomes detectably small even to consumers, so that there is a competitive equilibrium among dishonest dealers that yields virtually the honest price per measure delivered.

Not all fraud and opportunistic behavior can, or should, be eliminated if information is costly to obtain. The cost of deception and dishonesty is borne because specialization of production is so productive that usually it is better to turn to a specialist that is not quite trusted than to rely on oneself to mess up the task in a perfectly trustworthy fashion.

Knowledge is itself unique to particular circumstances, as Hayek[7] has observed, knowable more easily to those who find themselves in these circumstances than to those who plan without direct contact to these circumstances. In a real *laissez-faire* economy, acting upon knowledge possessed only by some requires exchange among voluntarily cooperating specialists. Hayek's conclusion, that decentralization is the superior method for incorporating knowledge into planning, however correct it may be empirically, is difficult to deduce once the costs of specialization, or of decentralization, are recognized. At least it is difficult to deduce if decentralization is carried to its conceptual limits. The costs of transacting and of the unreliability of one's trading partner may be sufficiently high to discourage complete decentralization. In such cases, competition in the private sector, accommodating to the potential for opportunistic behavior when information is costly, may reduce the scope of decentralized markets by enclosing specialized activities within the bounds of firms.

None of these adjustments, all of which are consistent with *laissez-faire* competition, could be predicted from the perfect decentralization model. In that model, farmer Jones delivers a known quantity of wheat and receives in return its full market value; no guarantee is required, and he could not care less about how much wheat is put into a bushel by his neighbour. The functioning of most *laissez-faire* markets is not distorted beyond recognition by the perfect decentralization model, but there is no denying that many market practices and institutional substitutions for markets, such as the firm, find their explanations beyond the limits of the perfect decentralization model. Their rationale is rooted firmly in information and transaction costs. By the same token, there is no denying that competition in a *laissez-faire* setting offers a full bag of tricks for accommodating to these costs.

VII. Normative Ambiguities

Information and transaction costs, to this point, have been discussed largely from the perspective of economic science. Although normative phraseology undoubtedly has found its way into this discussion, my objective has been to show how behavior and institutional arrangements can be made sense of, once the confines of perfect decentralization are abandoned, and how much of this behavior serves the interests of consumers as a group. Whether such behavior should be tolerated, encouraged, or discouraged is a normative matter about which, I believe, there is considerably more ambiguity than economists generally realize. I will discuss this essential ambiguity in the context of monopoly and externalities. At certain points, particularly in regard to antitrust policy, I will state normative positions, but the reader surely will recognize from the discussion that such positions are a compound of analysis, empirical judgement, and faith. They could not be derived from economic theory alone (contrary to the implicit treatment of these issues in much of economic theory), even if there were complete agreement that policy should serve the interest of consumers or of efficiency.

A.   Price Setting and Monopoly

Information and transaction costs often make

firms unique in time, place, and capabilities. Difficult to imitate, distinctive bundles of goods and services are offered to consumers by different firms in the "same" industry. In a fully adjusted long-run equilibrium, these distinctions as well as price differences, are undermined by competition. However, in the partial equilibrium of a given interval of real time, there can be no doubt that price setting capabilities are possessed by many firms. The quantities sold by firms do not fall to zero should they raise price slightly. The supply of perfectly substitutable goods and services is less then infinitely elastic during a time interval long enough to include price policy decisions.

The time consuming nature of imitation partly reflects underlying information costs. But it also reflects the legal rules governing competition in a *laissez-faire* economy. Such rules define the bundle of property rights contained in an ownership entitlement. The rules adopted by the legal system generally prohibit one seller from infringing on the ownership rights of another seller, where these rights include his entitlement to a unique identity. Imperfect substitutability among sellers and their goods results from this prohibition whenever brand names or seller identity convey information. The rationale for such a prohibition is to encourage investments in reputation and invention by making it difficult for the gains from such efforts to be appropriated by "free riders" who merely copy. The incentive to invest now for profit later is maintained through grants of patent, trademark, and copyright that bar this form of opportunistic behavior. These help to define what is owned by whom.

These legal barriers in conjunction with information cost allow firms and their products to differ for meaningful periods of time. A modicum of price setting capability therefore exists in a *laissez-faire* economy. This price setting capability, since its source is in real information costs or in legal rules designed to encourage efficient investment, may not be inconsistent with consumer sovereignty. A normative viewpoint about monopoly rests not only on some criterion, such as efficiency, but also on how that criterion is met over the entire spectrum of consumer wants. Consumer wants for presently available goods may be more amply satisfied by greater product homogeneity and less price setting capability, but, in the context of free riding opportunistic behavior, consumer wants for new, more reliable goods may be served better by limiting imitation. The choice, from the perspective of consumer sovereignty, is not whether sellers should compete but which competition is worthy of emphasis - competition among existing goods on a price basis or competition among different, and emerging, goods, on an innovative and reputational basis.

Although the quantitative significance of scarcity creating monopoly can be debated, there is no principle of *laissez-faire* that rules out its possibility. There may be successful collusion for a meaningful period, and there is the possibility of exclusive owner- ship of a unique, scarce resource. But even these types of monopoly are affected by information and transaction costs. If these costs, which for brevity we may call "exchange cost", were zero, the profit maximizing monopolist would *not* produce a lower rate of output than would the same industry organized in a perfectly decentralized manner. Exchange cost is the only impediment to fashioning a price tariff more complex than the single, uniform price usually assumed when discussing monopoly. Zero exchange cost allows the monopolist to adopt multipart tariffs, all-or-nothing price offers, and a variety of other selling arrangements that increase both his output and profits. If exchange cost truly were zero, it would be profitable for him to produce at a rate equal to that which would have been produced in the absence of any power to set price. Output would be at a level such that marginal cost is equal to the market demand for the good. The consequence of monopoly then would be purely distributional. The wealth of the firm's owner relative to that of consumers would be increased compared to what it would have been with a uniform, single price, and also compared to what it would have been if there were no market power. There would be no resource allocation effect except to the extent that the distribution of wealth affects the relative demands for goods. The "deadweight" *allocative* loss usually associated with monopoly simply cannot be deduced from the monopoly model under conditions of zero exchange cost.

Of course, exchange cost is not zero, so such fine tuning of price schedules and contractual arrangements is not possible. Since positive exchange cost bars the monopolist from discriminating costlessly in his selling activities, attempts by him to increase output must also reduce some of the prices that he could receive were he to maintain a smaller output rate. In the limiting case, with exchange cost so high as to allow only a uniform price to all buyers, monopoly does imply a smaller output rate than would be produced if the industry were organized in perfectly decentralized manner. Monopoly, in this limiting case, also implies that the monopolist's wealth is not as high as with zero exchange cost, although it may be higher than if he possessed no market power.

The "deadweight" allocative loss seems to reappear when exchange cost is significant. But the very existence of positive exchange cost makes invalid the logic that associates this reduced rate of output with inefficiency. That logic offers the equilibrium of the perfect decentralization model as a realistic alternative. However, since that equilibrium derives from the assumption of zero exchange cost, it ceases to be a relevant alternative. The oft-asserted inefficiency of monopoly is based on a comparison to the standard of perfect decentralization, a standard that is theoretically derivable only under the very conditions denied by the existence of a monopoly-caused deadweight loss.

If the assumption of significant exchange cost is applied to a decentralized industry, the conclusions derived from the perfect decentralization model no longer necessarily follow. Significant exchange cost implies that not all consumers will abandon a firm that raises its price, because it is costly for them to search out and transact with other firms. The frictions of the market place disallow instantaneous, complete reassociation of consumers and firms when price differences arise. Equilibrium, at least in the short-run, might be described better by some type of monopolistic competition model, perhaps adorned with Cournot type reaction functions. It is not entirely clear how the equilibrium of such a model would compare with that of the monopoly model. A convincing assessment of the allocative and distributional effects of market power, compared to realistic alternatives, requires more than a simple comparison of the monopoly and perfect decentralization models.

The existence of price setting capabilities, whether originating from benign imperfections in substitutability or from causes that seem to have no justification in terms of broadly guaged consumer sovereignty, implies that firms that exchange with each other have an additional reason to establish some control over the behavior of their exchange partners. Such controls can reduce the inefficiencies associated with the well-known "successive monopoly" problem. A manufacturer with some price setting capability has a wealth incentive to prevent a distributor of his good, also possessing price setting capability, from reselling at a price in excess of the distributor's marginal cost. A high distributor price mark-up reduces the quantity that the manufacturer will sell at any given price of the manufactured good. For similar reasons, the distributor has a wealth incentive to see to it that the manufacturer's mark-up is as small as possible. Should these two firms act completely independently, each operating at a rate where "own" marginal revenue equals "own" marginal cost, their joint profits *and* consumer welfare will be less than if they control each other's excesses. This becomes transparently clear should they merge, for then the distributing end of the business will receive the manufactured good at its true marginal cost, not a price that contains a price-setters mark-up. The vertically integrated firm will produce more, ask a lower price of consumers, yet increase its profit as compared with independent maximizing efforts by separate firms. This result is also achievable, entirely or in part, by the exercise of control over each other's pricing and/or output policies while not engaging in full vertical integration.

Imperfect information creates a demand for

information about product quality and production technology, but also about prices. Beginning with Stigler's important article on the economics of information,[8] a substantial literature on optimal search for price information has emerged. In Stigler's analysis, for example, a key role is played by amount to be spent on purchasing a good. For any given marginal cost of search, search for a lower price will be carried further the more expensive is the good being purchased. This implies that a normalized measure of the variation in market prices above the mean price will tend to be smaller for high price goods than for low price goods. This body of recent research is too large to summarize here, but two important implications of it reveal the difficulty of prescribing public policy toward business.

First, given positive search costs, it is possible for there to emerge a stable distribution of different prices for a homogeneous good, a conclusion impossible to derive from the perfect decentralization model. The mere existence of different prices for what seems to be the same good, therefore, need not imply that pricing practices harmful to consumer interests are being pursued. Secondly, risk averseness on the part of sellers and buyers attaches a positive value to reducing uncertainty about prices. It is not surprising that we observe trade associations whose primary objective is the gathering of price information. This information, of course, may be useful to sellers seeking only to collude. but it may also be useful to sellers merely seeking to improve their competitive investment and productions plans. Such knowledge, by reducing uncertainty about the current state of affairs, for risk averse sellers at least, leads to an increase in output, other things being equal. The potential output restricting effect of such knowledge, therefore, may be offset by the output increasing effect of reduced uncertainty about present conditions. Consumers also may find superior a market characterized by less price variance, and, hence, less need for search, even if accompanied by a somewhat higher level of average price. More price information tends to make production less risky and shopping less costly, but more price information also tends to make tacit collusion easier. These contrary effects pose a difficult problem for antitrust policy toward trade associations.

B. Antitrust

Competition in the *laissez-faire* economy will yield a wide variety of buyer-seller "vertical" pricing arrangements, virtually all of which benefit consumers. On occasion, such competition will also yield discriminatory price schedules, and these, in general, also result in greater output for any given degree of monopoly. *Laissez-faire* competition also can be expected to create industry structures that are skewed when underlying cost conditions call for unequal distributions of output among the firms in an industry; such skewness also works to the advantage of consumers. The *laissez-faire* economy may experience episodes of successful price collusion, and these may be more likely in highly concentrated industries, or in industries well organized through trade associations. On rare occasions, through luck, ability, or merger, one firm may acquire control of an important resource. In these cases, the interests of consumers may not be well served.

This variety of possibilities confounds the task of antitrust policy. The welfare of consumers would not demand that price setting capability be attacked wherever found, for much price setting is desirable and inevitable, nor would consumer interests call for a broad attack on industrial concentration, for much concentration is competitively justified. And, given the inevitability or desirability of some price setting capability, discriminatory pricing policies often improve the welfare of consumers. Antitrust must distinguish between situations more likely to harm than to benefit consumers.

The ambiguity and vacillation that have marked the U.S. experiment with antitrust reflects the conflict between an interpretation that sees antitrust as a policy against all price setting capability and an interpretation that asks antitrust authorities only to promote consumer welfare. The first interpretation is impossible to execute. Antitrust cannot substitute for business pricing decisions nor can it regulate the private enterprise system. The second interpretation, given what I have already said, is difficult to execute. Its basic premise is that beneficial competition in the private sector is naturally robust, so that antitrust need tend to only a relatively few aberrations. This interpretation suggests there is wisdom in adopting a few basic permissive and prohibitive policies, eschewing any attempt to fine-tune *laissez-faire* competition. Two permissive policies seem desirable:

1.   Price reductions and various vertical pricing and marketing practices should be allowed.

2.   Vertical, conglomerate, or other nonhorizontal mergers should be allowed.

These two permissive tenets would prevent antitrust authorities from interfering with practices very likely to promote efficiency and consumer welfare. The U.S. experience has been marked by repeated attempts to prevent some firms from harming other firms through price cuts or through (contractual) agreements that restrict somewhat the freedom of action of vertical exchange partners. The result has been to protect competitors, not to protect competition that would benefit consumers. Additional policies, more prohibitive in nature, that seem desirable, are the following:

3.   Search out and strike at price fixing and market division agreements.

4.   **Consider** blocking horizontal mergers only if

this keeps an industry from becoming very concentrated, but **allow** an efficiency defense of such mergers.

5. **Consider** restructuring an industry when there exists a highly dominant ownership of an important resource (not dominance in the product market) for which little cost justification can be found.

These three prohibitions are sufficient to root out those aberrant cases in which *laissez-faire* competition is unlikely to serve the interests of consumers. If the anti-consumer aspects of *laissez-faire* competition are considerably more severe than is envisioned by such a policy, then antitrust alone cannot resolve the monopoly problem. I believe there is ample evidence of the robustness of beneficial competition. It can be found in per capita living standards, in the strong tendency for equalization of profit rates over time, and in the frequency with which established market positions are upset by rivals. Combined with a free trade policy, such an antitrust policy, in my opinion, goes farther than the recent policy of the U.S. in disciplining *laissez-faire* competition to favor consumers.

C   Externalities

The relevance of the cost of exchange to the theory of externalities was completely neglected until

R.H. Coase wrote his important article "The Problem of Social Cost" [9] two decades ago. Coase argued that if exchange cost is zero, the private cost of an economic activity must equal its social cost, so that the root source of the externality fails to exist. Moreover, once positive exchange cost is treated explicitly in the analysis of externalities, the standard normative conclusions about how to correct externalities cannot be deduced without empirical judgements exogenous to the theory.

The source of the externality problem is the scarcity-caused competitive demands for the use of resources. However, to recognize the existence of competitive claims is also to recognize the existence of incentives for negotiations to take place between those who wish to put a given resource to competing uses. The private property system, through ownership entitlements, establishes who it is that controls the use of resources, and, therefore, who must pay whom to influence the use to which these resources are put. Negotiations will take place as fully as exchange cost allows. If this cost were truly zero, as it is imagined to be in the perfect decentralization model, all potential gains from negotiating would be fully realized.

Suppose that the owner of a factory, as part of his rights, owns the right to manufacture with techniques that result in smoke and soot, and that these techniques are less costly for him to use than is some alternative clean fuel. If he uses soft coal, soot will dirty the home of a neighbor. With this definition of rights, the neighbor has an incentive to offer the factory owner a payment to substitute clean fuel for coal. The neighbor would be willing to pay an amount up to that which equals the damages he suffers from the soot. The factory owner requires a payment no less than what would be sufficient to cover the additional cost to him of using a clean fuel.

Negotiations between the two must resolve their conflicting interests in a manner that maximizes the value derived from the scarce air space that both seek to use. If the damage that would be done to the neighbor by soot exceeds the damage that would be done to the factory owner by switching to clean fuel, then negotiations must result in the elimination of the soot. Since soot is removed when the cost of its presence exceeds the cost of its removal, the value secured from the use of scarce air space is maximized. The cost to the neighbor of the factory owner's use of soft coal is no longer external to the factory owner's calculations. It is reflected in his calculations as an *implicit* cost of continuing to use soft coal.

Of course, if the cost of switching to clean fuel exceeds the cost of soot to his neighbour, the factory owner will not be offered enough by his neighbor to induce him to switch to clean fuel. The cost of soot still enters the factory owner's calculations, so it is not external to his maximizing behavior; but, by assumption, it is insufficient to make clean air the highest value use of air space. Air space in this case, is more valuable as a medium for transporting soot. Arithmetic assumptions about the relative magnitudes of the costs of acting one way or another with respect to the use of air space will alter the negotiated outcome, but zero exchange cost implies that no cost of an activity will be external to deciding whether or not to undertake it. No divergence between private and social cost is possible in a regime of zero exchange cost, so that competition necessarily allocates resources to their highest value use.

Moreover, the efficient use of a resource, from the perspective of consumers of the resource, is the use that will be dictated by these negotiations no matter who owns the right to control the cleanliness of the air. If the property right system defined homeownership to include the right to sootless air in the vicinity of the home, then the factory owner, wishing to use soft coal, would need to negotiate with his neighbor for the neighbor's permission to put soot into the air. The outcome of these negotiations again depend on the arithmetic of the relative costs, but this arithmetic is the same as when the factory owner owned the right to use soft coal, so the use of the air space will be the same. If it is assumed that the cost of soot to the homeowner is less than the cost of clean fuel to the factory owner, then the factory owner will succeed in purchasing from the homeowner the right to put soot into the air. If the cost of soot to the homeowner exceeds the cost of clean fuel to the factory owner, the negotiation will fail and sootless air must result. The use of air space is thus the same with either definition of property rights if the cost of exchange is zero.

The distribution of wealth, however, differs. If the factory owner owns the right to use soft coal, the homeowner must pay to encourage a switch to clean fuel; if the homeowner owns the right to sootless air, the factory owner must pay for permission to put soot into the air. To the extent that this income distribution affects the relative demands for clean air and factory goods, the choice of owner will alter, to some extent, the use of air space. But that use always is efficient in terms of the underlying distribution of wealth.

If the cost of exchange is positive, some negotiations of the sort discussed above will not take place and the allocative effects of the specific system of property rights will begin to show. In the extreme case of prohibitively high exchange cost, there will be no negotiations, with the result that soot will be more plentiful if factory owners have the right to use soft coal than if the homeowners have the right to sootless air. Divergences between private and social cost reappear, but now it is not longer possible to draw the usual normative conclusions.

If exchange cost is zero, there is no divergence between private and social cost. The allocation of resources efficiently conforms to relative demands and costs in the economy. If there is exchange cost, so that with one definition of property rights there is

H. Demsetz

more soot than with another definition, it is no longer apparent which definition maximizes the value of air space. A standard such as is explicit in the analysis of externalities - that resources should be used efficiently - provides no guidance, because the dictates of consumer sovereignty are not determinable without market revealed values. We cannot suppose such knowledge, or what action it calls for, merely because curves and numbers can be placed easily on classroom blackboards. The critical importance of market provided information cannot be ignored. The absence of such information must undermine our confidence as to which use of resources conforms most to consumer sovereignty when externalities are relevant. Alternative sources of information are available, but at a cost. These include cost-benefit analysis and preferences for resource allocations as expressed in the polling place. Consumer interests are not reflected accurately through these alternatives; political and research sovereignty are substituted for consumer sovereignty. In practice, this may produce solutions not tailored well to consumer interest. Yet, even these techniques often are rationalized as methods for improving on the market's ability to serve consumers.

Positive information cost implies that unforeseen events will create new rivalries for resource use. Thus, a technological development that allows the construction of large buildings, or of aircraft, creates new competing demands for the use of lower air

space.   The   primary   institution   of   *laissez-faire*
responsible for settling these disputes through an
official definition of private rights is the court
system. The definition chosen by the courts will have
wealth consequences for the contending parties. That
is why there is a rivalry to secure entitlements. The
definition   will   have   consequences   for   resource
allocation also, because the cost of exchange is
positive.

Suppose that it were true that most persons
desirous of building tall structures attach greater
value to each foot of building height than do
neighbors   whose   view   will   be   blocked   as   a
consequence. Were the courts to award the right to a
view to these neighbors, their wealth position would
be improved relative to what it would have been if
the court had given builders the right to construct tall
buildings.   Under the assumed definition of rights,
builders would pay for permission to build taller
structures.   However, for some builders, the gains
from going higher, although exceeding the value to
the neighbors of their views, would not exceed this
value to enough to cover the cost of exchange.   In
these cases, the building's height would stop short of
what it would be if the court had instead given to
builders the right to construct tall structures.   The
efficient decision in such a case calls for the builders·
to receive the right.   If this decision had been made,
fewer resources would be absorbed in the exchange
process and fewer buildings would be held to low

heights when the cost imposed on neighbors would be
worth bearing from the perspective of consumer
sovereignty.

It is, of course, possible to assume that the
contrary is true, that neighbors attach greater values
to their views than builders, or than the occupants of
their buildings attach to greater height. If such were
true then exchange cost could be reduced and views
worth preserving could be protected by awarding the
entitlement to the neighbors.

If the court system were to auction off the
entitlement, property rights would tend toward
definitions consistent with consumer sovereignty. To
this there are two caveats. First, if one of the rivals
is better positioned to exercise monopoly power were
he to own the contested entitlement, he might bid
more for its ownership even if consumer sovereignty
were not better served by his ownership. Second, the
awarding of an entitlement confers benefits to all
similarly situated contestants, whether or not they
appear to bid; thus if builder A submits the highest
bid in court, he wins the entitlement not only for
himself but for others who have a comparative
advantage in building. There will thus be a tendency
to "free ride" on bids made by others. The bidding
process would not work perfectly for these reasons.
Problems of monopoly and externalities are not
irrelevant to the functioning of the court system.

The present process, which eschews such bidding,
is not guided by any obvious criterion to cater to

consumer welfare. Facts are presented, arguments are
made, and the court decides. Often the decision
accords with earlier precedent, but sometimes not.
The equivalent of a profit test, such as is used to filter
decisions and actions in the market place, seems to be
absent.

The problem is made tolerable because a decision
to award an entitlement to a party who cannot put
the resource to its highest value use, as determined
by consumers, will be bought into that use through
the market once the rights are defined by the court
system. Nonetheless, on the margin, an incorrect
court decision uses more resources than need to be
used to bring the resource into a use that caters to
consumer sovereignty. The principle of seeking an
efficient definition of rights is not in conflict with
court guidelines, however. These envisage a
"blindfolded" justice that refuses to see the wealth,
sex, or color of the supplicants before her. Only facts
are supposed to matter. The only remaining facts are
the costs and benefits of the courts' decisions and the
precedent that is applicable.

The possibility does exist for a series of court
decisions to evolve an efficient precedent. An
incorrect decision, by definition, imposes more cost
on the class of persons situated similarly to the losing
contender than it confers gains to the class of persons
similar to the winner. Losers, in such a situation,
have greater incentives to seek redress. Thus, if
builders as a contending class of similarly situated

persons lose more than is gained by neighbors when
the court awards the right to a view to neighbors,
then the decision will be contested more frequently
and forcefully than had the court decided in favor of
the builders.   The implicit market for redressing
decisions will be more forceful when earlier decisions
have undermined consumer welfare.[10]   Common law
court procedures, it may be argued, increase the
likelihood that an efficient precedent will survive.

It should be noted in passing, when exchange and
information costs are significant, redefining ownership entitlements is not without its cost. I refer here
not merely to court cost but to consequences for the
efficiency with which resources are allocated.   The
maintenance of an efficient stock of productive assets
is dependent upon the expectation than an ownership
interest will persist. If exchange and information cost
were zero, owners-to-be, in the case of redefining the
ownership of entitlements, would be known, and it
would be in their interests to pay present owners to
make the proper investments. Such transactions are
barred by uncertainty and positive exchange costs,
especially for owners to be who are not yet born.

VIII.   Concluding Comment

I have discussed competition in the *laissez-faire*
economy in the spirit of the political philosophy of
laissez-faire, preserving to non-market institutions,
except for antitrust, only the function of defining

and defending private rights of action. Competition in such a setting creates institutions, such as business firms, and pricing and exchange practices, such as "vertical" price control, that are explainable only when information and transaction costs are allowed to adulterate the pristine conditions of the perfect decentralization model. Some degree of price setting capability must arise from such competition, but much of it, from a broad perspective, is in the interest of consumers. At times, monopoly and externalities, or more accurately, exchange cost, will blunt the preferences of consumers. Yet, I believe that the *laissez-faire* economy is very responsive to consumer interests. Indeed, *laissez-faire* is more effectively objected to when it *does* respond to consumer preferences than when it does not. The operation of a free market is interfered with frequently because some consumption preferences, well serviced by the market, offend the tastes of large numbers of people. This is irrelevant in a *laissez-faire* economy because minorities and majorities are not a meaningful distinction in that setting. But it is a distinction full of portent for competition in the public sector. In that sector, to which I now turn, voters may censure the consumption habits of their fellows.

FOOTNOTES

[1] R.H. Coase, "The Nature of the Firm," **Economica,** IV (1937), 386-405

[2] A.A Alchian and H. Demsetz, "Production, Information Costs, and Economic Organization," **American Economic Review,** LXII, 1972, 777-795.

[3] This explanation of vertical integration is discussed by A.A. Alchian, R. Crawford, and Benjamin Klein in " Vertical Integration, Appropriable Rents and the Competitive Contracting Process," **Journal of Law and Economics,** Vol. 21, No.2 (1978), 297-326.

[4] A more detailed exposition of this explanation for vertical price restraints is given by Lester G. Telser, "Why Should Manufacturers Want Fair Trade?", **Journal of Law and Economics,** Vol. III, 1960, 86-105.

[5] On this proposition, and for supporting evidence, see H. Demsetz, 'Industry Structure, Market Rivalry, and Public Policy," **Journal of Law and Economics,** Vol. XVI, 1973, 1-10; H. Demsetz, "Two Systems of Belief About Monopoly," in **Industrial Concentration: The New Learning,** Edited by Goldschmid et al., 1974, Little Brown; S. Peltzman, "The Gains and Losses from Industrial Concentration," **Journal of Law and Economics,** Vol. XX, 1977, 229-265.

[6] See Benjamin Klein and Keith B. Leffler, "The Role of Market Forces in Assuring Contractual Performance," **Journal of Political Economy,** Vol. 89, No. 4, 1981, 615-641.

[7] F.A Hayek, "The Use of Knowledge in Society," **American Economic Review,** Vol. 35, 1945, 519-30.

[8] G.J. Stigler, "The Economics of Information" **Journal of Political Economy,** Vol. LXIX, No. 3.

[9] R.H. Coase, "The Problem of Social Cost," **Journal of Law and Economics,** Vol. III, 1960, 1-44.

[10]Paul H. Rubin, "Why is the Common Law Efficient?", **Journal of Legal Studies,** Vol. VI 1977, 51-64; a forthcoming paper by B. Klein, K.M. Murphy, and G. Priest, "Litigation v. Settlement: A Theory of the Selection of Tried Disputes," presents another view of the outcome of the Common Law process.

Lecture 3

COMPETITION IN THE PUBLIC SECTOR

I. Introduction

Although political systems have been discussed at least as long as have economic systems, and very probably longer, progress toward a general theory of their functioning has been noticeable only in recent years. Knowledge about the operation of economic systems has come at a faster pace for basically two reasons. The first, and less important, is that economics possesses, in money, a very useful common denominator by which to compare economic phenomena. The second is our willingness to accept and grant free rein to individual self-interest when thinking about narrowly defined economic behavior. Until very recently, students of political behavior have often been unwilling to make such a commitment, assuming instead a significant public interest motivation.[1]

The issue here is one of quantitative significance. Very few economists would deny that altruism plays a role in economic behavior, but, however interesting specific cases of such altruism may be, still fewer economists would contend that it is a quantitatively important component in economic behavior. The issue is the same for political behavior. Quantitatively, how much political behavior is motivated by altruism? Or, an even more important question, how much political behavior can be **explained** by postulating altruism? The tardy development of formal political science suggests that the self-interest postulate could be put to useful purpose in matters of politics.

Motivation, in any case, has little to do with the success of politcal behavior. Politcal democracy, when effectively competitive, filters out bureaucratic behavior that displeases voters, whether altruism or narrow self-interest has motivated voters. Politicians who indulge only their own prejudices soon join the unemployed or some college faculty.

Competition subjects politicians and political parties to the filter of the polling place, much as competition subjects managers to the filter of the market place. The analogy is stated well by Joseph Schumpeter:

> '..... the social meaning or function of parliamentary activity is no doubt to turn out legislation and, in part, administrative measures. But in order to understand how democratic politics serve this social end, we must start from the competitive struggle for power and office and realize that the social function is fulfilled, as it were, incidentally − in the same sense that production is incidental to the making of profits.[2]

Voter sovereignty, expressed through ballots, replaces consumer sovereignty, expressed through dollar votes. The personal preferences of political professionals are no more relevant to democratic institutions, when political competition functions well, than those of businessmen are to *laissez-faire* when economic competition functions well. A reduction in the effectiveness of competition in either regime tends to separate the survival of functional agents from the control of their formal constituencies. Carried far enough, the absence of political competition undercuts the democratic content of political institutions.

The consequences of the competitive pursuit of self-interest in domocratic politics is the central concern of this lecture. It is useful to begin the discussion with a political counterpart to perfect economic decentralization; this may be named "Perfect Political Democracy".

II. Perfect Political Democracy

Perfect political democracy assumes there are no informational or transactional costs to acting politically. These costs, to distinguish their field of application from market exchange, may be called "voting cost". The assumption that voting cost is zero is analogous to the assumption that exchange cost is zero in the perfect decentralization model.

The major difference between perfect political

democracy and perfect decentralization lies in the nature of individual ownership entitlements. In perfect decentralization, most wealth is privately owned and may be sold in open markets. In perfect political democracy, there is only a private right to vote. This right may not be sold openly, but it can be cast for programs designed to benefit the voter, and, in practice, many votes are secretly sold. To this basic difference may be added more or less arbitrary rules of political decision, such as the common one requiring that the preference of the majority of voters is what determines political policies and programs. In perfect political democracy, the voting majority calls the tune. Any person desirous of hearing a different melody must emigrate, if he is allowed to by his fellow citizens. Voting majorities determine political outcomes, and all outcomes are political.

Neither constitutional roadblocks to majority preference nor the existence of a parallel private sector can be assumed. If they exist, they are a result of political choice. Such a choice is highly plausible in a democracy. Everyone will prefer to exercise personal control over some resources, so virtually everyone would be willing to concede personal control to others in order to obtain some for himself. Perhaps more important, the majority will be willing to create and protect private rights to wealth, even for those not in the majority, if this encourages production from which the majority will benefit; if we superimpose on perfect political democracy the right of every individual to refuse to work, such protection should be forthcoming.

Citizen owners of entitlements to vote will use these to maximize their individual welfare. All voters are *potential* gainers if they cast their votes to reject inefficient political programs, but the majority of voters are sure gainers because they stand to receive some or all of the increment to output value that remains after compensating those whose voluntary efforts are required to achieve efficiency. In a situation in which there is full information and no cost of acting politically, there is nothing to bar the majority from achieving this result (setting aside problems of cyclical voting and strategic behavior). The reasoning is the same as that which argues that private property rights, in this case the right to vote, will be exercised efficiently if the cost of exchanging entitlements is zero and if there is full knowledge of opportunities for deploying resources. In such a setting, political policies can always be devised to pay voters for voting in a desired manner. The avoidance of inefficient political programs provides the wherewithal for such compensation.

The most important similarity between perfect political democracy and perfect decentralization is that in both no individual exercises authority or wields control over others. No single voter can control events. Nor can a single politician. The most significant difference lies in the exercise of authority by a majority of voters in perfect political

democracy.   No such authority exists in perfect
decentralization.   Individuals operating through
markets may offer to buy and sell without securing
the permission of others.   This distinction derives
from the absence of a unanimity voting requirement
in democracy.   Not every voter's agreement is
necessary to implement policies, even policies to
which all voters will be subjected.

And there must be some political programs that
impact all voters.   If the concept of a nation has
meaning, there must be important government
activities consumed by the entire population.   A
nation cannot offer a multitude of foreign policies,
one to suit each voting faction, nor can it possess two
different defense establishments.   Government
policies such as these require that the entire
population consume what winning voters choose.
Many political choices need not be so uniform over
an entire population, in which case political decisions
can be left to local communities (or to markets).

In contrast, under conditions of perfect
decentralization, the assumption of sharply rising
marginal cost guarantees that no penalty is paid by
consumers who purchase different products than do
others.   However, in a *laissez-faire* economy,
economic decentralization may sometimes yield to
scale economies.   When it does, the price an
individual pays for a good will reflect how many of
his fellows join him in purchasing that good; [3] buyers
become dependent on others, much as a voter

becomes dependent on how many other voters favor the policy that he desires. There remains a distinction, however. The individual consumer can acquire a good, providing he is willing to pay the price, whether or not other consumers also desire the good; the individual voter needs the co-operation of others if he is to receive a desired policy from the government. Even a casual look at the market place and the polling place reveals that the individual is vastly more dependent on the agreement of others in political democracy than in *laissez-faire*. The power of the majority must be reckoned with in democracy. In perfect political democracy it prevails completely. Indeed, the proper test for imperfections in democratic institutions lies in the extent to which majority interests are defeated.

III. *Imperfect Political Democracy*

Voting costs are not zero. Indeed, the information cost of ascertaining one's political interests are quite substantial. Voting cost alters the consequences of competition in political democracy, much as exchange cost alters the consequences of competition in the *laissez-faire* economy. But the costs of becoming informed and of acting politically are not simply a political variant of exchange cost. They differ qualitatively and quantitatively because of the authority of the majority in elections.

It is widely acknowledged by students of

democratic institutions that voters will not acquire much knowledge about political issues and candidates. Nor will they greatly exert themselves to apply what knowledge they possess. This is so much so that, often, the outcome of an important election turns on as trivial a matter as where it will snow and rain and where it will not. The disincentive for an individual to invest in the political pursuit of self-interest results from the diminimus impact of such an investment on political outcomes. A political outcome that surely alters the wealth of a typical voter by $1,000 would not lead him to invest nearly that much in informed political action because it is not *his* vote alone that determines public policy. The institution of democratic politics, through the authority of the majority, by preventing each vote from having much impact on political events, impairs voter incentives to learn and to voice political self-interest.

By comparison, a decision in the market place, where the choice of a product will alter the value of a consumer's utility by $1,000, is likely to encourage considerably consumer investment in product knowledge. His dollar votes determine what he purchases, and, in the absence of scale economies, the price he pays for what he purchases is independent of the behavior of other buyers.

This contrast between *laissez-faire* and imperfect political democracy is important but somewhat overstated. In imperfect democracy, the minority possess power to influence outcomes in two ways at least. As is emphasized by Buchanan and Tullock, [4] a majority may concede to a minority on an issue of secondary importance to the majority in return for support from the minority on some other issue of more importance to the majority and on which its dominance is less clear. This log-rolling or vote trading conveys power to a minority, but it does so only when the majority is less dominant on other issues. The second path of minority influence, discussed by Stigler[5], is in reducing the size of the voting gap between the majority and the minority. A majority possessed of only a one per cent plurality is less able to dictate policy than is one enjoying a twenty percent plurality. The strength of the minority vote signals how lightly the majority must tread if it is to remain the majority.

The issue raised by these considerations is the incentive possessed by the individual voter to become politically informed and to vote. His incentives are greater because his vote does contribute to determining the relative strengths of majority and minority in influencing policy. It is a mistake, however, to equate this increase in the voter's incentive to become informed about and act upon his alternatives to the incentives that he has as a consumer. The use of a given amount of time and the expenditure of a given sum to search among market alternatives yields a much greater expected increase in welfare to a person consuming in the market place than to the same person consuming through the polling place. In the market place his purchase may be tailored closely to his taste. In the polling place he will need to be satisfied with a compromise that his vote has influenced very little. Politics is the art of compromise because political outcomes are very indivisible. The greater divisibility of market outcomes makes business the art of serving new wants without compromising old ones.

The size of the voting gap between majority and minority is no doubt important in influencing the political compromise that emerges from democratic politics, but it should not be confused with proportional influence. When 15 per cent of consumers desire small automobiles, the market will tend to devote 15 percent of its output to small autos. In a two party democracy, a minority possessed of so few votes as 15 per cent is not likely to influence political outcomes by as much as "15 per cent"; indeed, its influence will be difficult to discern. As the minority increases its vote to, say, 40 per cent, its influences will grow. But probably not to the point where it will carry a 40 per cent weight in determining political outcomes. Minority parties can exercise more power in multiparty democracy, sometimes so much power, as when a minority party possesses the swing vote necessary to determine which major party shall govern, that proportional weighting is destroyed from the other extreme.

The greater rational ignorance of voters to which these differences between representation in the market and in the polling place give rise has important implications for political competition. These are discussed next. Where possible, the discussion is related to consequences of exchange cost for market competition.

A. Political Institutions

There would be little reason for political parties to exist if political democracy were perfect. A party presumably brings a particular perspective and consistency to political problems. The party's common political philosophy integrates different political programs. However, any interaction between various programs could be resolved costlessly and directly by voters through any desired number of referenda if democracy were perfect. Positive voting cost bars continuous voting by a fully informed electorate. The cost of providing full information to voters in separate elections for each combination of candidate and issue is so great that intermediaries are necessary. These are political parties. They play a significant role in the competition of imperfect political democracy by assembling issues and candidates and by offering general political positions to voters. The function of the political party in imperfect political democracy is somewhat like that of a firm in the *laissez-faire* economy. The political party, intent on pursuing its interest, combines candidates and issues much as a firm combines inputs, and offers these to voters in competition with other parties. The party attempts to reconcile differences in the preferences of its constituency, much as a firm attempts to design products that suit the differing needs of its customers.

B.   *Opportunistic Behavior*

A serious problem faced by political parties is that of creating and maintaining the confidence of voters. In the absence of full information, voters no longer can be sure that promises will be kept. I suspect that they are often sure that they will not be kept. The attempt by parties to combat disbelief is not easy or costless. One cost is the great difficulty they have in adjusting quickly to unexpected developments in the political environment. The Democratic party in the U.S. has long championed income redistribution, requiring high taxes, or inflation, and extensive welfare programs. The recent rebellion of taxpayers in the U.S., unexpected in strength, has swept the Republican party into office. The Democratic party cannot wrest control back from the Republicans simply by redesigning its program to cater immediately to the new political environment, not given that it has been promising redistribution for five decades. Such opportunism would undermine confidence in its willingness to deliver on future promises. It is therefore forced into a partial and slower adjustment to the new environment. The notion that opposing political parties can quickly move to near identical programs, as in Hotelling's spatial competition model, is fallacious.

Competition by political parties to maintain voter confidence is likely to be more difficult that it is for business firms to establish confidence among consumers. Business firms are *owned*. Political parties are not. The wealth of owners of the specialized assets of firms is positively correlated with consumer confidence in the goods and services they produce. A *known* breach of that confidence is visited upon owners of firms through the resulting decline in the value of their assets, so they have a powerful incentive to avoid such breaches. The same incentive cannot function so strongly on political parties because no one's wealth is tied so closely to a party's performance by virtue of his simply being in the party or even a leader of it. A party member's career in politics might suffer as a result of his or some other party member's breach of voter confidence, but the cost of a political party's failure to deliver a subsidy or a tax reduction is borne primarily by would-be receivers, not by members of the party. The cost of a known failure by a private firm to satisfy quality and delivery agreements made with buyers is borne by the firm through a combination of damage claims and reduced demand for its products. The stock market quickly evaluates the impact of these on the value of ownership shares when these shares are traded publicly. By the same token, although exceptionally good performance by a political party surely benefits a political party and its members, it also delivers much of the benefit to outsiders. The benefits of fulfilling a promise to reduce unemployment are captured mainly by the unemployed, not by the political party.

The fortunes of political parties and their members, then, are more poorly correlated with performance than are the fortunes of owners of firms. Even when political parties are turned out of office by voters, the impact of the defeat is not concentrated on party leaders. As a result, we may expect the leaders of political parties to control fraud and deception less effectively than do owners of business firms. For the same reason, quite aside from the problem of reducing fraud and dishonesty, achieving the goals of political programs is likely to be more difficult for a party than achieving business objectives is for a firm, assuming in each case equally severe competition.

Private ownership of political parties, which might establish similar lines of responsibility, is not practical. Once parties win elected posts, they make decisions that affect the welfare of all citizens, not just those citizens who voluntarily might have purchased an ownership share in the party. Citizens, or at least a minority of them, must abide by the policies of a winning party whether or not they are beneficiaries of these policies. Unlike consumers, who may buy or not buy from a particular firm, citizens may be *forced* to pay taxes that are primarily used to improve the welfare of party owners. The right to coerce more funds from citizens, a right derived from majoritarian rule combined with voting cost, makes for a much more powerful conflict of interest between a party and taxpayers than can possibly exist between the management of the business firm and those who supply its capital. After all, it is more difficult for citizens harmed by political programs to leave the nation than it is for buyers of goods to turn to rival sellers, or for owners of corporate stock to sell their shares. The political method for resolving this conflict is to bar private ownership. One cost of this solution is to weaken the correlation between political performance and the personal wealth of politicians. The result is an increase in shirking, fraud, and political ineffectiveness. Political competition cannot easily cater simultaneously to the problems of conflict of interest and shirking. Outright ownership of parties seems to pose unacceptable risks to the electorate, even if private wealth is used to influence candidates and parties.

Voting cost leads to packaging of programs over time as well as across political parties at any given time. Elections are too costly to experience very often, not merely because electioneering and voting are costly. Many national policies require the passage

of time before their success or failure can be
determined, and many programs require a
commitment to others that has an important time
dimension. Infrequency of elections allows working
time, but it also reduces the rapidity with which
voters may directly discipline their parties. Business
firms are disciplined by consumers on a continuing
basis. The impact of poor quality or of dishonest
performance is felt quickly by firms once it is
discovered; revenues available from sales or from the
capital market are soon made more difficult to
secure. While exchange cost may delay somewhat
consumer reaction, the pause will be very brief.

Quantitative differences are important here, for,
ultimately, political parties are also disciplined. This
is quicker in regard to resources that are voluntarily
contributed. But the time period between elections is
long enough to provide governments with a delay
before voters actually withdraw publicly provided
resources. The desirability of providing governments
with time to work out their programs comes at the
cost of an increase in the probability that politicians
will behave opportunistically, taking advantage of the
delay in reckoning. The infrequency of elections
encourages more short-run opportunistic behavior
than the continuity of economic competition permits
to business firms. Adam Smith writes eloquently on
the quantitative importance to opportunistic behavior
of frequent competitive encounters.

Whenever commerce is introduced into any country, probity and punctuality always accompany it. These virtues in a rude and barbarous country are almost unknown. Of all the nations in Europe, the Dutch, the most commercial, are the most faithful to their word. The English are more so than the Scotch, but much inferior to the Dutch, and in the remote parts of this country they (are) far less so than in the commercial parts of it. This is not at all to be imputed to national character, as some pretend. There is no natural reason why an Englishman or a Scotchman should not be as punctual in performing agreements as Dutchmen. It is far more reduceable to self-interest, that general principle which regulates the actions of every man, and which leads men to act in a certain manner from views of advantage, and is as deeply implanted in an Englishman as a Dutchman. A dealer is afraid of losing his character, and is scrupulous in observing every engagement. When a person makes perhaps 20 contracts in a day, he cannot gain so much by endeavouring to impose on his neighbours, as the very appearance of a cheat would make him lose. Where people seldom deal with one another, we find that they are somewhat disposed to cheat, because they can gain more by a smart trick than they can lose by the injury which it does their character. They

whom we call politicians are not the most
remarkable men in the world for probity and
punctuality.   Ambassadors from different
nations are still less so: they are praised for any
little advantage they can take, and pique
themselves a good deal on his degree of
refinement.   The reason for this is that
nations treat with one another not above
twice or thrice in a century, and they may gain
more by one piece of fraud than (lose) by having
a bad character.   France has had this character
with us ever since the reign of Louis XIVth, yet
it has never in the least hurt either its interest or
splendour.[6]

C.   Interest Groups

The gains and costs that result from rational
political ignorance are neither randomly nor
uniformly distributed. The effective political pursuit
of self-interest by voters who are organizationally
isolated or who have no great personal stake in the
politcal issue being debated is severely hampered,
while the political advantage of organized special
interest groups is enhanced. The steel industry and
its workers, for example, are active in seeking and
securing political protection from imports.   They
learn their interest in such protection and they are
willing to act on that interest because the benefits
from protection are concentrated on the relatively

few who invest and work in the industry. Their incomes are significantly affected. The larger costs of their protection are borne in dispersed fashion by the much more numerous population of taxpayers and consumers. The dilution of cost renders its bearers politically ineffective.[7]

The political power of special interest groups stems not only from the ease with which politcal programs whose benefits are concentrated on them can be implemented, but also from the lower cost of organizing their efforts. This cost is lower because members of such groups are normally in contact with each other during much of the working day. Dispersed individuals, even though they share the same politcal interest, face larger organization costs. These they will overcome only when the psychic or financial return for doing so is much greater than is required to mobilize organized special interest groups.

A politician competes to be elected whether his behavior is analyzed in the framework of perfect or imperfect political democracy. In perfect political democracy his election depends only on his conformity to the wishes of the majority of voters in his district, but in imperfect political democracy the line of dependence is less clear. The probability of election still depends on the interests of the majority, interests which they neither know clearly nor pursue actively. But victory also depends on the human and financial resources available to a condidate or his party. Such resources may be used to convince the broad constituency in his district that their interests are his and his party's. Campaign resources often find one of their main sources in narrow constituencies. Frequently, these are economic interest groups, such as the steel industry, but sometimes they are ideological constituencies.

The ideological constituency may be held together by organizational glue somewhat weaker than that which binds an economic interest group, and ideological constituencies may lose frequently when competing against economic interest groups. But often the opposition faced by an ideological constituency is the general interest, not some narrow economic interest, and, against this opposition it has power disproportionate to its membership. No small portion of this power is exercised propagandistically on the majority, but much of it is brought to bear on the government. And even ideological politics have their narrow economic interests. Such groups, because of their organizational cohesiveness, carry greater weight in imperfect political democracy than their number would grant them in perfect political democracy.

The isolated, individual voter has little incentive to pierce the propagandistic veil spun by these or by industry based groups during and between campaigns. He is more the dupe in the polling place than in the market place. In markets his interests are sharpened by the fact that his money payment determines what he purchases. Of course, he does not always betray his self-interest when he votes, if he does vote, and, when it comes to tax cuts, his interest may be easier to kindle. Nonetheless, he serves the interests of specialized groups more often than their numbers would merit in perfect political democracy.

The problem of organizing and achieving political representation for the general public interest is great, but it is insignificant in comparison to the problem posed by democratic politics for future generations. The "yet to be born" face an infinitely large cost of directly turning political democracy to their interest. Not possessing the franchise, they are forced to rely on competition between living voters to serve them.

This is also true of competition in the *laissez-faire* economy, but competition in the market place is much more likely to serve future generations than is competition in the polling place. The profit maximizing market calculations of resource owners serve the interests of the future in ways that have no practical counterpart in democracy. Those who seek maximization of private wealth through markets attempt to forecast accurately the prices that present *and* future generations will be willing to pay for specific uses of owned resources. Anticipation of a rapidly growing future demand for lumber leads the present owner of land to fell fewer trees and to plant more, because he anticipates a rise in the price of lumber that exceeds the prevailing interest rate. Resource owners, pursuing their own interests, represent future interests in today's marketplace. They are properly viewed as brokers, auctioning the use of their resources, not only to those presently alive, but indirectly to the future also. By virtue of a choice to inventory a resource, even to augment its supply, they implicitly give representation to future consumers. Intellectuals who dwell on problems of externalities when criticizing the ability of markets to protect future generations often fail to examine the political alternative. Their view of a growing private forest is obscured by smoke from some factory, quite possibly from one owned by the government.

Today's voters, were they to decide to set public resources aside for the use of future generations, could have but little confidence that future voters would respect their decision. The political process functions on the basis of constituency preferences, not legally binding entitlements. Even the self-denying ordinances of political constitutions give way before the interests of succeeding generations of voters. No individual voter can profit directly from a political choice to set resources aside. He has no ownership claim on such resources. Nor can he profit future generations, because he cannot individually *or* collectively create a binding constraint on the treatment of resources by future political constituencies.

Political machinery lends itself to the production of collective goods, such as national defense, the rule of law, and assorted programs to ameliorate (or worsen) externality type problems. It does so because it is a superior institution for coercing people to do or to contribute to doing that which they would not individually volunteer to do. But this capability is more admirably suited to the task of redistributing wealth among those now alive. In the provision of collective goods government can make only the roughest of guesses as to proper objectives and how to accomplish these, especially when concerned with the distant future. Goals and methods are much clearer when it comes to near-term wealth redistribution.

Such wealth redistribution, aside from the duties of a limited, *laissez-faire* government, are the major activity of modern governments. One important effect of this activity is to diminish present incentives to invest, because the future private income derivable from investment may be subjected to political redistribution. Wealth acquisition through redistributive political processes competes with wealth acquisition through investment; the more government is used for redistribution, the more investment will give way to consumption, leisure, and the seeking of political influence. The asset base that is passed on to future generations would *seem* to be made smaller than it would otherwise be because of the political propensity to redistribute wealth.

Price controls may temporarily transfer wealth from those who seek to sell goods to those who succeed in buying them, but the resulting diminution in incentives to invest falls ultimately on future consumers. The redistribution of wealth from apartment owners to renters, when rents are controlled, reduces the incentive to invest in maintaining and increasing the future stock of apartment buildings. The cost ultimately falls on future renters, who confront a smaller stock of apartments than would have been available to them in the absence of rent control. In the U.S., the energy program has continuously played to pressures for wealth redistribution, and usually at the expense of the future consumer; supplies of new crude oil have been sacrificed to the demand that oil profits be taxed and petroleum prices be held down. With regard to environmental regulation, wherein the interests of future generations would seem to be served, what is surprising is how long it has taken for democratic politics to bring such problems forward, and how much the treatment of these problems caters to the ***present*** interest of environmental groups, such as the Sierra Club in the U.S., rather than to the real interests of future generations.

It would also ***seem*** to be the case that the median voter of future generations should desire much less present wealth redistribution. If the future generations could vote today, not knowing whose sons or daughters they were to become, they would have no interest in present wealth redistribution, or at most, their interest would be limited largely to the purchase of insurance against delivery to excessively poor parents. Political activity for redistributionist purposes, then, hardly can be viewed as catering to the interests of the representative future generation. The reduced rate of per capita growth in income in those democracies that have succumbed most to redistribution (England, for example), is consistent with political inattention to the future. The incessant din of present calls for wealth redistribution makes it difficult for politicians to hear the pleas of future generations. In the political arena, those generations bear a considerable competitive disadvantage.

However, the systematic bias in favor of those now living is difficult to discern in the totality of political behavior because special interest legislation often moves government to undertake activities that apparently benefit future generations. The use of taxes to subsidize the education of children of middle income voters yields an investment in human capital, but since these children would, in the main, have been educated anyway, public education primarily is an income redistribution program in which the poor and the wealthy subsidize the middle class. The political power of trade unions and construction companies pressures government to construct very durable facilities, whether these be interstate highways or school buildings. If the work is done correctly, these facilities are sure to be available for many years to come. These cross currents of special interest legislation make it difficult to detect the neglect of future generations. What can be said, however, is that the political allocation of resources deviates from that which would obtain if all future and present voters could cast time discounted ballots.

D. Monopoly

If monopoly were to be assessed on the basis of market concentration, it must be judged to be greater in the political sectors of Western Democracy than in their unregulated economic sectors. The number of major political parties that dominate the political scene is generally smaller than the number of major firms in an unregulated industry. Frequently, only one or two political parties hold most of the offices in legislative bodies. In the twenty year period from 1932 to 1952, with the exception of one Congress, the Democrats in the U.S. firmly controlled both the Administration and Congress, and, even after losing the presidency to Eisenhower in 1952, again with the exception of one Congress, they contined to control Congress until 1980. In no major unregulated U.S. industry has one firm been so dominant for so long.

Over this period, the median American voter clearly believed that the Democratic party best served his interest, and that would be all that is implied by such political dominance in the hypothetical world of perfect political competition. Costless referenda by fully informed voters could, in principle, keep the same party in office without suffering from an abuse of political power. Effective competition for the right to political leadership need not result in atomistically structured political institutions, for there seem to be significant indivisibilities in the exercise of political leadership, both at any given time and over time. With perfect political competition, the concentration of political offices in one or a few political parties is consistent with efficiency.

Imperfect political competition, both because of the infrequency of referenda and the rational ignorance of voters, conveys a measure of true monopoly in politics. Political outcomes, as a result, will differ from those implied by perfect political competition. This does not mean that real political institutions are inefficient given the constraints under which they necessarily operate. Rather, as in the *laissez-faire* economy, where firms do have some power over price, it means that the constraints are different than in a world in which information and transaction costs are assumed to be zero. Just as it would be incorrect to draw the normative conclusion that *laissez-faire* is inefficient when exchange cost bars the realization of the perfect decentralization equilibrium, so it would be incorrect to draw the conclusion that imperfect political democracy is inefficient when voting cost is significant. Realistic alternatives must be compared before one can conclude that improvement is possible.[8]

If normative judgements are difficult to make, it is nonetheless possible to ask how political power is

H. Demsetz

used. One case, already discussed, of the exercise of
power out of proportion to numbers, is that of
special interest groups. Another is found in the
power of office itself. The fact that special interest
groups receive political benefits out of proportion to
their number is more a reflection of the weakness of
the party in power than it is of its strength. A very
successful party, perhaps put in office by a political
rebellion of the tax paying majority, is in a position
to resist the interests of such groups, and, for a period,
at least, to compromise even the interests of the
taxpayers. Such a party has the power to benefit
itself.

In this context, it is useful to define the political
party as including not only its official membership,
but also the organized ideological constituency with
which it is identified. That constituency provides the
intellectual and material support to the party,
especially when it is out of office. When the party, so
defined, exercises its political power, it will do so on
behalf of office holders and ideological supporters.
When it gives special attention to outside groups, it
does so, not because it has political power, but
because these outside groups have political power.
The party itself will favor its ideals and programs over
other interests when conditions permit. In the main,
this means increasing salaries, more perquisites of
office, and indulgence in more authoritarian behavior,
all at the expense of dispersed taxpayers. It also
means raising barriers to political competition and

favoring   programs   desired   by   its   ideological constituency.

There have been several studies of voting patterns by Congressmen and Senators in the United States, especially in regard to how they have voted on issues related to political programs concerned with energy. These studies suggest that ideology benefits from the exercise of political power. There have been some clear outside economic constituencies that have been served, especially the subset of refiners that had relied on the use of domestic crude oil as feed for their refineries. For them for some time, domestic crude oil prices were held below world prices. But there have been considerable differences between the actual voting pattern in Congress and the pattern implied by the strength of economic interests in their districts and states. The best explanation of this deviant voting has been found in an ideological index. That index is how favorably a Congressman's prior voting record was judged by the Americans for Democratic Action. Deviations of their votes from voting patterns that would have been consistent with the desires of narrow special interest groups within their districts are very highly correlated with ADA index.[9] This indicates that a measure of monopolistic political independence is exercised by representatives on behalf of their ideological constituencies.

In summary, the political power that arises from voting cost, power that allows political outcomes to deviate from majority interests on specific issues, favors both narrow specialized interests and the political party itself, including its ideological constituency. At times these two beneficees will be in conflict. Which group wins when that conflict is important depends on just how dominant is the party in power. If its policies enjoy strong, broad-based support, the ideological constituency will be a more important beneficee of monopoly power than when the success of the party in office rests on a narrow vote margin. The ideological constituency has nowhere else to turn, other than to create a new party, so, grudgingly, it will continue to support its party even when the party finds it necessary to favor special interests over party ideology. Special interest groups, because they can switch allegiance quickly, will be the main beneficees of political power whenever opposing parties are closely matched.

FOOTNOTES

[1]Important in the incorporation of self-interest in models of the political process are the pathbreaking studies by Downs, A., **An Economic Theory of Democracy** (New York: Harper and Row, 1957), and Buchanan, J. and Tullock, G., **The Calculus of Consent** (Ann Arbor, MI: Ann Arbor Paperback, 1965).

[2]Joseph A. Schumpeter, **Capitalism, Socialism, and Democracy,** (New York: Harper, 1950), 282.

[3]This comparison between the constraints imposed by democracy on the individual voter and the constraints imposed by scale economies on the individual consumer is noted by George J. Stigler, "Economic Competition and Political Competition," **Public Choice,** XIII, pp. 93-106.

[4]**The Calculus of Consent, op. cit.,** footnote 1.

[5]"Economic Competition and Political Competition," **op. cit.,** footnote 3.

[6]A. Smith, **Lectures on Jurisprudence** (Cambridge University Press, 1978), 538-539.

[7]This point and the general view of political theory to which it gives rise are discussed in George J. Stigler, "The Theory of Economic Regulation," **Bell Journal of Economics and Management Science,** (1971), 3-21.

[8]On this general point, see H. Demsetz, "Information and Efficiency, Another Viewpoint," **Journal of Law and Economics,** XII (1), 1-22.

[9]Cf., Edward J. Mitchell, **Energy and Ideology** (Washington, D.C.: American Enterprise Institute, 1977); Joseph P. Kalt, **The Economics and Politics of Oil Price Regulation** (Cambridge, MA: MIT Press, 1981), 237-28.

Lecture 4

THE GROWTH OF GOVERNMENT

Highly organized groups, because their political power reflects an influence that extends beyond their numbers, generally prefer more, not less, government involvement in the affairs of society. This preference reflects the ability of special interests to shift the cost of what they want to others. Consider the problem of colluding. In the U.S.. the mere **attempt** to collude **privately** is illegal and, if discovered, puts violators at risk of paying punitive damages and even of serving jail sentences. If not discovered, the collusion still must be enforced and maintained at private expense, perhaps by pricing low enough to discipline a seller who deviates from the collusive agreement. The firms that cut price to teach the deviate a lesson must then suffer losses to keep the collusive agreement viable. The tendency will be to let someone else discipline the deviate, especially because such price cutting may be interpreted by antitrust courts as predatory. But there is no legal barrier to petitioning a democratic government for aid. Producers who combine forces to secure protection from competition through government regulation, therefore, may do so without fear of violating antitrust laws. Such protection, if they secure it, is enforced by the government at taxpayer expense, and enforced with much more coercive power than the colluders could exercise privately.

As a general proposition, then, organized groups, whether they be unions, trade associations, or the education establishment, have a general interest, on average, in favoring intervenionist government policies. The diffuseness of taxpayer and consumer interests allows the bill for such intervention to be shifted to them. On the *margins* of this political struggle, it is not always easy to judge when special interests will overpower the general interest. The larger is the fraction of income that is already taken from the diffuse majority, the more difficult it will be to take yet more away. Taxpayers do rebel. Within the framework of democratic institutions, the limits to the magnitude of such transfers appear to be below 50 % of official GNP figures (and below a smaller percentage of true GNP). The diffuse majority who pay the taxes seem capable of reasserting control when that large a fraction of their income is diverted through government programs. But it is only during the last forty years that such limits have been reached in Western industrialized nations. Throughout most of the modern history of these nations, the fraction has been much lower. Yet, it has grown steadily since at least the turn of the century. Why this trend?

The preference of organized groups for interventionist policies helps to explain this steady

growth, once proper account is taken of the industrial
revolution. One of the most important consequences
of the industrialization of the West has been to
increase specialization of production and
employment. This has created new and more
numerous highly organized interest groups, and, in
turn, a steady upward trend in the demand for
interventionist programs. Creeping socialization of
Western economic systems has resulted. The relative
growth of the government sector, perhaps the outstanding political development of the last century, is
a normal response to growing demands for
redistributionist programs, and these have had a good
part of their origin in the increasing specialization of
economic activity that has been both a cause and a
consequence of the Industrial Revolution.

So important a development as the widespread
growth of government sectors in political
democracies has attracted both attention and
explanation. The explanation given above, rooted in
the increasing specialization of economic activity, is
but one among many. Some of these others are
excessively mechanical, as when the relative growth
of government is based on ratchet effects. Thus,
government is enlarged to cope with war or recession
but is destined never to return to previous relative
size; "Once the rascals are in, they cannot be thrown
out," is not much of an explanation as to why voters
who endorsed government growth cannot manage to
bring about its shrinkage. Even though several

Western nations have experienced large war time growth of government, there also has been fairly steady moderate growth during years of peace. Moreover, even those Wesetern nations that have successfully avoided wars, such as Sweden, have also experienced rapid growth of the government sector.

Some explanations give large weight to the power of particular personalities, such as F.D. Roosevelt in the U.S., or to the force of important ideas, such as those of Keynes. One is inclined to ask why *these* men and *these* ideals succeeded rather than competitors and their ideals. In any case, it is difficult to use such an explanation for trends beginning as early as the turn of the century in England and but a decade or two later in the United States. A continuing succession of men and ideas favoring centralization would be required, and for this there would need to be additional explanation. Nor will the Great Depression suffice to explain trends that began before and continued after the decade of the 1930's. Such explanations are at best short-run, and as such they cannot convincingly rationalize what has been essentially a persistent phenomenon for six to eight decades.

Bureaucratic behavior is given center stage in still other explanations. These tend to stress the desire of bureaucracies to substitute growth for the profits prohibited them by political institutions. Implicit in such a theory is a power of voters to prevent profit maximization from guiding political behavior. This would seem to be an extremely difficult task since profits are so easily disguised; yet, in this theory, these same voters appear powerless to prevent behavior that causes bureaucracies to grow, a much easier task since bureaucratic growth is an easily observed phenomenon.

There are explanations of growth based on government's widely recognized role as a redistributor of wealth. I do not deny the importance of this role, and have, in fact, underscored it in the third lecture. But why this activity should expand persistently remains the essential unanswered question. One would need to assert the presence of underlying non-government forces that continue to create ever larger "maldistributions" in wealth that require evermore "corrective" action by government if the explanation for growth of government is to rest primarily on its role in seeking more or less inequality in the distribution of wealth.

These explanations, and others not discussed here, may rationalize government growth at particular times, and taken together their explanatory power may increase. Nonetheless, they do seem ad hoc and prone to view government growth as beyond the control of the polling place.

A convincing explanation of the trend in government growth must be consistent with political competition and it should reasonably account for the *two* important features of the historic pattern of changing government sectors in the U.K. and the

U.S., and to lesser extent, in other democratic industrialized nations.

1. Between 1750 and 1850, especially in the U.K. and the U.S., the relative size of government sectors generally *failed* to grow.

2. From the late 19th century to recent years, the relative sizes of government sectors grew steadily in most democratic industrialized nations.

The standard explanations of government growth cannot easily accommodate the first of these historical patters. They are silent about the period of *laissez-faire*, to the point even of failing to recognize the need for explaining this substantial period during which there was no growth (in the U.K. and the U.S., at least) in the relative size of government sectors. The explanation of government growth that I have stated earlier, based on political competition in a setting where the industrial revolution causes an increasing fraction of economic activity to become specialized, must also explain these two somewhat inconsistent patterns. The evidence may be evaluated briefly here in regard to the U.K. and the U.S.

During most of the period from 1700 to 1900 Western nations created a social and political atmosphere that tolerated and protected the amassing of private wealth holdings. The response was the creation through private risk taking of new *specialized* industries, often employing large labor forces, frequently in new tasks. Specialization of activity within large firms, and new specialized industries, were the hallmark not only of Adam Smith's *Wealth of Nations* but of the wealth of nations. The fact that an *ever increasing* fraction of the economy became specialized during the industrial revolution must have meant that the political opportunities for securing government protection were also growing. The barrier to effective political action that is raised by voting costs is more easily overcome by specialized interest groups. The industrial revolution brought about an economy containing more such groups. The effective political demand for protection rose and so did the growth of government at the end of the 19th century.

The more puzzling part of the history is why government growth began well after the industrial revolution had been underway. The apparent move toward *laissez-faire* between 1750 and 1850 seems inconsistent with an explanation of government growth based on increasing specialization of econmic activity. As a factual matter, the 100 years between 1750 and 1850 do not reveal the decline in relative size of government that one might expect from a move to *laissez-faire*. If the years occurring during and around the Napoleonic Wars are struck from U.K. data (see Table 1), the remaining years reveal a rather stable size of government relative to national income 1792 − 11% , 1841 − 11%, 1850 − 12% , 1860 − 11% , 1870 − 9% , 1880 − 10%, and

TABLE 1

U.K. GOVERNMENT EXPENDITURES AS A PERCENTAGE
OF GNP

Year	Veverka Estimates Total	Peacock and Wiseman	
		Total	Excluding Interest and Military
1792	11%		
1800	24		
1814	29		
1822	19		
1831	16		
1841	11		
1850	12		
1860	11		
1870	9		
1880	10		
1890	9	8.8%	5%
1900	15	14.4	6
1910		12.8	8
1920		26.1	11
1928		24.2	13
1933		25.9	16
1938		30.1	16
1950		39.5	26
1952		41.9	24
1955		37.3	22

Source: Peacock and Wiseman, **The Growth of Public Expenditures in the United Kingdom** (NBER, Princeton University Press 1961), pp. 37, 42, and calculated from Appendix tables.

1890 — 9 %. Scattered U.S. data also indicates a relatively constant share of resources allocated to government during this period, approximately 6 to 7 percent of GNP (see Table 2). Constant shares during

TABLE 2

U.S. FEDERAL, STATE AND LOCAL EXPENDITURES AS A PERCENTAGE OF GNP

Year	Percentage of GNP		
	Total	Federal	Nonfederal
1902	6.8	2.4	4.4
1913	8.0	2.4	5.6
1922	12.6	5.1	7.5
1932	21.3	7.3	14.0
1940	20.3	10.0	10.3
1950	24.7	15.7	9.0
1960	30.1	19.4	10.7
1970	34.1	21.3	12.8

Source: **Budgets and Bureaucrats**, Thomas E. Borcherding, (ed.), (Duke University Press, Durham, NC., 1977), p. 26.

a period of growth in total and per capita incomes, however, implies a rapidly growing absolute size of government. From a quantitative perspective, it would not seem to be true that the relative sizes of government sectors in the U.K. and the U.S. decreased during this 100 year period, and these sectors certainly increased absolutely. In Germany and France the relative size of the government sector during the 1800's and early 1900's appears to have grown somewhat.

Still, an explanation for the lack of *growth* in the *relative* size of government sectors during the "take-off" period of industrialization is in order. Two reasons may be given. (1) The move toward fewer market restrictions was consistent with industrialization because the market restrictions eliminated were not primarily those protecting new industries, but those protecting the specialised interests that *preceeded* industrialization. (2) There are reasons for expecting that political action soliciting protection will not be (as) actively sought sought by industries faced by favorable growth prospects, and the emerging industries of the industrial revolution did enjoy such prospects.

During the 16th and 17th centuries what specialization existed in England was largely identified by craft or by merchant, and sometimes these specializations were captured in the legislated distinctions maintained between towns and rural areas. The division of interests between these specialized groups and consumers provided foci in these earlier years for legislated intervention in private transactions. This earlier species of government activity responded to the interests of a pre-industrial society. Roadblocks to the free flow of labor were created by this earlier legislation. Migration between towns and from rural areas into towns often was restricted by legislation that forced labor to remain occupied in rural industries and agriculture. Crafts and Guilds operated under protection of lengthy and legally enforced apprenticeship requirements.

Such protection hardly could be useful to the new industries that emerged during the industrial revolution. If these industries had any interest in these protective measures, it must have been largely a negative interest. Greater mobility of labor was what they sought. There was no constituency of growing importance that sought to maintain this fabric of interferences in labor markets. More to the point, the new industries, by creating demands for new skills or (to work power looms) for the unskilled, simply made these restrictions largely inapplicable and irrelevant. Laborers became more mobile and less subject to restrictions because new occupations replaced old ones. During the middle third of the 19th century, the vestiges of this pre-industrial government protection, for which there no longer was strong support, were struck down in a legal sense, but the objective of this iegislation probably had been secured well before this. To quote from Mantoux (1961):

> Both these sets of regulations (Statute of Artificers and Acts of Settlement), together with the rules of dealing with industrial technique and with the provision of the Poor Laws, were part and parcel of one whole, a characteristic monument of traditional legislation. In the middle of the eighteenth century this edifice was still standing, though much decayed and battered. But it was to be soon shattered, more by new interests than by new ideas, and the workers tried in vain to prop up its crumbling ruins.[1]

The atrophying of these constraints did move English society toward less government involvement in markets, but not by stripping *new* industries of protection. Indeed, some new industries began to acquire protection during this period, a process that accelerated later but was overshadowed by the striking down of older restrictions.

The slow growth in the regulation of the new industries reflected their strong growth potential. With capacity well below expected long-run demand there was little incentive to restrict output. Even a monopoly would have sought new capacity. Moreoever, the large but still unsatisfied markets for these new industries is a rough index of the popular opposition to restrictions on growth. Hence, the effective political demand for protection emanating from the new industries was relatively small during the first part of the 19th century.

The demand for protection that existed early in the industrial revolution also faced a reluctant supplier of such protection. Parliament was still dominated by agricultural and rural interest. Parliamentary representation reflective of the industrial revolution lagged behind the reality of that revolution, largely because the franchise was still highly limited. Democracy did not emerge full blown from the shrinking powers of the monarchy. A substantial extension of the franchise waited upon passage in 1884 of Gladstone's Franchise Bill which virtually provided manhood suffrage — only those of no fixed abode, domestic servants, and bachelors living with their families were excluded. Some 2 million voters were added, nearly four times the number added in 1832 and twice the number added in 1867. Prior to this Bill, democracy in the U.K. was highly limited and biased in favor of landed interests. Electorates were small — at Marlborough, Wells, Thetford and Knaresborough, for example, they were less than 300 in 1865. Even Birmingham with a population of nearly 300,000 had less than 10,000 voters. The extension of suffrage during the last decades of the 19th century in England was in fact partly at the urging of industry which saw in its workforce political interests similar to its own. By the end of the century the union movement won for itself the legal right to organize and strike. This did open a conflict with industry in regard to wages and working conditions, but as for tariffs and subsidies, interests still coincided.

As to international trade, the interest of many of the new specialized industries in England often favored trade liberalization. Reducing English tariffs on foreign grains could reduce the real cost of labor to such industries by allowing for a larger growth in labor supply. Perhaps more important, such tariff reductions might lead to reciprocal reductions in foreign barriers to the exports of English manufacturing industries. These were industries that had developed early leads over foreign competitors in the adoption of specialized and mechanized methods of production. The liberalization in international trade after the middle of the 19th century was aided by the end of the Napoleonic wars and the beginning of reductions in international tensions. Trade tends to be liberalized when international tensions lessen and to be protected when tensions heighten. This is not different from but is directly related to the phenomenon of specialization. A nation that produces a full spectrum of products has little reason to fear that the outbreak of hostilities will leave it without some important economic resource or capacity. Increasing specialization of economic activity, therefore, will increase the correlation between public tolerance of free trade and the prospects for peace.   It is safer to become more dependent on neighbors when at peace with them.

Under Huskison, Peel and Gladstone, free international trade achieved a level of development in England that was never to be equalled again.   It culminated with the signing of the Cobden treaty with France in 1860 which substantially reduced or ended "all duties on manufactures."   England enjoyed unparalleled prosperity during the two decades beginning in 1850. World trade centered on England, and she led the world in many key industries.   But it became clear that other nations were by no means prepared to forego protection when the treaty system of the sixties collapsed. England still held to free international trade, but calls for protection mounted at home.   These came primarily from agricultural interests and from industries producing clocks and watches, hats, boots, gloves, silks and ribbons, woollens, shipping, and iron.

The great move toward protection began after 1875 as the factors that had moderated the demand for and supply of protection began to reverse themselves. As the industrial revolution progressed in Europe, the new industries of England met stiffer competition from maturing counterparts on the Continent. The market's potential no longer clearly exceeded the capacity to supply the market. Tariff barriers began to mount.   Faced with robust competition on both sides of the channel, the natural interests of rivals was served by a division of markets through tariff barriers. The move toward protection received help from an earlier recession and from the threat posed by Bismarck's growing influence in Europe. It was not until international frictions mounted early in the 1900's that England abandoned its international policy of free trade. The seeds for that event were clearly sowed in 1895, when the protectionists succeeded in putting Joseph Chamberlin into the post of Colonial Secretary. The essential elements of Chamberlin's subsequent tariff reform movement was largely the work of manufacturers who suffered from foreign competition and foreign tariffs.

After 1900, it became clear that the interests of specialized groups were in accord with the seeking of protection from competition, but it should not be thought that protectionism for the new industries had not been on the increase prior to this. The shift toward tariffs, toward legislative approval of unions (as labor became ever more specialized), and a host of minor measures since 1870, and earlier, reveal that protectionism had never really died. The cotton industry, for example, was protected against imported printed cottons. Sometimes protectionism meant the establishment of standards of employment with regard to age, sex, and hours, where these served to protect uneconomic, non-mechanized shops from the competition of larger factories. The government also moved steadily from a position of freeing labor markets from older restrictions to one of granting new restrictive powers to organized labor. Between 1870 and 1900, the impact of increasing government involvement in the markets and the operation of the new industries began to become evident. The steady increase in the involvement of government in the affairs of new industries had been hidden behind the destruction of an extensive edifice of earlier protectionism and by the rapid growth of the private sector. The collapse of protectionism for the craft, guild, and agricultural interests was sufficiently important, and the expansion of output was sufficiently great, that the **relative** size of the government sector failed to increase until the turn of the century.

The American colonists brought with them the English common law tradition, but they did not institute the type of legislation, such as the Statute of Settlement, that erected serious barriers to the free flow of labor; in a frontier setting, such legislation, even if desired, could not be enforced. The colonies, then, did not inherit a substantial portion of the legislation that had protected the preindustrial specialized activites of England. The United States, born of suspicion and fear of central government, partly because of the commercial and fiscal policies of England toward her colonies and partly because the separate states jealously guarded their political power, offered greater resistence to an enlargement in the role of central government than did England. The emotional, psychological, and political dimensions of the American Revolution gave real strength to a policy of decentralization and limitation of political power during the 18th and 19th centuries. While it is difficult to measure fully the resources controlled by the separate states, the size of the government sector in the United States relative to national income appears to have been slightly more than half the relative size of English government during nonwar periods of these 200 years.

Toward the end of the 19th century this *laissez-faire* environment began to crumble. The famous case of Munn v. Illinois (1877) allowed regulation to extend to property "affected with a public interest". In this case, the court upheld the right of the State of Illinois to fix maximum charges collectable by privately owned grain elevators. It is difficult to reasonably construe "affected with a public interest" in this case as anything but the existence of interdependence arising out of specialization. Such an interpretation suggests that this decision removed all legal constraints to extended government involvement in economic matters. The precedent was quickly applied to industries not previously thought subject to price regulation under the common law. But these extensions were sporadic and unsystematic. The reliance of shippers, especially of agricultural products, on railroads give birth to state laws in the Midwest. The Granger Laws sought to regulate the commercial interface between these interests. The first major Federal intervention to regulate prices reflected the attempt to resolve this at a different political level.   The Act to Regulate Commerce, 1887, marked the beginning of a pattern of regulation based on alleged dependencies born of specialization.

In agriculture also, it was primarily *commercial* crops, those whose value was determined on centralized organized exchanges — cotton, and tobacco, and wheat, that benefitted from subsidies and parity prices. It is instructive to quote from the decision in U.S. v. Rock Royal Cooperative (1939), a case which legalized the right of the Secretary of Agriculture, under the Agricultural Marketing Agreement Act of 1937, to fix minimum prices to be paid for milk.

> The people of great cities depend largely upon an adequate supply of pure, fresh milk.   So essential is it for health that the consumer has been willing to forego unrestricted competition from low-cost territory to be assured of the producer's compliance with sanitary requirements, as enforced by the municipal health authorities.   It belongs in the category of commodities that for many years has been subjected to the regulatory power of the state.

The specialization of milk production for shipment to large *dependent* cities could hardly be used to support such legislation in 1800, because there was no specialization, but it could be 1937. Similarly, the Supreme Court in the Sunshine Anthracite Case (1940), when upholding the right of a Federal Commission to establish minimum coal prices under the Bituminous Coal Conservation Act of 1937, used the rationalization that "If the strategic character of this industry in our economy and the chaotic conditions which have prevailed in it do not justify legislation, it is difficult to imagine what would." In more recent years, it has been this fear of relying on specialized suppliers outside the U.S. that has been used successfully to rationalize the protection accorded the U.S. petroleum industry.

The last twenty years of emphasis on general income redistribution has brought the size of governments to new peaks, but it is a development not easily rationalized through increasing specialization of economic activity except in the psychological sense of increasing sensitivity to the broad social interdependencies created by a specialized economy. But these broad redistribution programs, in any case, seem to be in full retreat across Western democracies (with the exception of old age security programs).

We may ask whether the long term trend of government growth will resume and carry Western democracies to the point of reducing private sectors to insignificance. There is no doubt that political competition disadvantages the large majority who still represent diffuseness of interest. The individual who is not a member of a highly organized interest group is financially disadvantaged by political competition. The larger the relative size of the government sector, the greater is his disadvantage. Under *laissez-faire*, a person's income, after deducting the relatively moderate tax payments required to run a limited government, is determined largely by the value of his marginal product and by the time he gives to working. His tax payment presumably delivers to him an average amount of benefit from the legal and defense services provided by a limited government. Under imperfect political democracy, if he is typical of the many unorganized taxpayers, he must also pay taxes to support a wide variety of programs devised to aid highly organized, politically effective interest groups. From these programs he derives little or no benefit.

The typical taxpayer has little incentive to understand or resist the political demand for wealth redistribution when the public sector is still so small as to impose only a modest tax burden on him. His interest in what is happening surely grows as greater numbers of organized petitioners for government aid succeed in raising his tax burden. The gains to organized political groups, however, should fail to increase in proportion to his burden. There will be increasing amounts of slippage as resources are transferred through a large government bureaucracy, one that is by its very nature prone to a high degree of shirking behavior.

Where the equilibirum is struck between the opposing forces of taxpayers and organized interest groups, and the precise mechanism used to establish the equilibrium, is difficult to ascertain theoretically. At some juncture, one would expect, the increase in taxpayer concern, combined with the ineffectiveness of the bureaucracy, will somehow outweigh the organizational advantages possessed by specialized by specialized interest groups. The surface evidence of the last century, if it is a useful guide to the future, suggests no common limits to the relative size of government in a democracy. Imperfect political competition in a democracy, since the industrial revolution, say since 1920, *seems* tolerant of a wide range of government sizes, with official measures varying between 10 and 60 percent of GNP. The latter number is characteristic of the Netherlands, Norway, and Sweden in recent years, but Japan and Switzerland maintain governments that are much smaller than this. The former number, 10 percent, is characteristic of the United States and the United Kingdom in 1920, but as recently as 1955 there were many industrialized nations in which size of government was equivalent to less than 30 percent of GNP.

The apparent variability in the relative size of governments cloaks a much smaller real range than these official figures suggest. As the relative sizes of government sectors grow, so do the unrecorded sizes of the hidden private sectors that operate beyond the reach of tax authorities. These hidden sectors have grown quite large in high tax rate nations, that is, in those nations with relatively large public sectors. Recent estimates report underground economies equal to at **least** 25 percent of official GNP for nations with relatively large government sectors, and not less than 10 percent of official GNP for nations with moderately large government sectors. Since underground economies are relatively more important when government sectors are large, an adjustment that more realistically measures total economic activity would tend to reduce the real upper limit of the relative size of government by more than it reduces the lower limit. If these estimates are used to correct the official numbers, the real relative sizes of contemporary government sectors would seem to vary in industrialized democracies from a low range of 25 to 30 percent of real GNP for Japan and Switzerland, to a high range of 48 to 50 percent for the Netherlands, Norway, and Sweden. France, the United States, West Germany, and the United Kingdom occupy the range between 35 to 45 percent of real GNP.

An equilibrating process seems to be at work, but it is based on two mechanisms, political opposition at the polls and avoidance of taxes through underground transactions. Underground economies as large as those that have developed recently are relatively new upon the democratic scene, precisely because relatively large government sectors in democracies are a post World War II phenomenon. Current developments seem to be making underground sectors more important, not less. The tendency to "free ride" on taxpayers is found not only in organized special interest groups, which realize their goals through the political process itself, but also in the individual, whether or not he is a member of such groups, who realizes his goals through underground transactions. His behavior in this respect faces less political and personal hindrance than might be supposed. The cost he imposes on taxpayers is so diffuse that there is little incentive for mass political opposition, and many of the services provided by government may be those which the individual is unwillingly forced to provide by organized special interest groups. He can compensate for his disadvantage at the polls simply by avoiding the official economy. The natural source of political opposition is in the organized special interest groups, whose "collective" desire is for greater government expenditures. But since these groups are made up of individuals who also seek to avoid taxes through underground transactions, this opposition cannot be strong. The underground economy in a democratic society, therefore, is difficult to control.

In the nondemocratic industrialized nations of Eastern Europe, the underground sector is probably half the size of official GNP. Moreover, it seems that the maintenance of minimally acceptable living standards in these countries requires unofficial toleration of the underground economy, so even non-democratic nations seem incapable of supporting government sectors larger than 65 percent of real GNP.

Competition in the private sector and in the public sector would not seem to be independent parameters. Internal checks and balances seem to be at work. As private sector competition spills over into the political competition of imperfect democracy, the relative size of the government sector seems capable of increasing from 10 percent to, say, 25 percent of GNP before the feedback system of underground transactions starts to become significant. The feedback becomes more forceful as the government sector increases beyond 30 percent, making the size of that sector difficult to push much beyond 45' percent of real GNP in a democracy. This suggests that the tolerable range of contemporary real government sectors in democracies is contained between 30 and 45 percent of total real GNP. In a more peaceful world, the upper limit might be still lower, perhaps under 40 percent of real GNP.

There is not yet enough experience to determine whether democratic political institutions are compatible with governments as large as 40 percent of real GNP. The politics of confrontation seems to characterize organized political competition when the government sector gets that large. Organized groups are not much inclined to take the political parameters of democracy as a given and beyond their control.

This form of competition may turn out to be too disruptive to remain within the bounds of stable democratic institutions.

FOOTNOTE

[1]Paul Mantoux, **The Industrial Revolution In The Eighteenth Century**
(New York: Harper & Row, 1961), rev. ed., p. 452.